SISTER KATE

Kate O'Hanlon spent sixteen years as sister in charge of A & E at the Royal Victoria Hospital in Belfast during the most violent period of the Troubles in Northern Ireland. She helped treat the victims of bombings, shootings and punishment attacks such as the Malvern Street shootings of 1966, the loyalist bomb attack on McGurk's Bar, the IRA bombing of the Abercorn Restaurant, the car-bombing in Donegall Street which saw 150 casualties arrive, and Bloody Friday. Gun battles occasionally spread into the grounds of the hospital, and Kate would find herself ordering police and soldiers out, while stopping crowds of people from forcing their way inside, afterwards sharing a brandy with her shaken colleagues. Through it all, she held her team together with warmth, compassion, humour, and an indomitable spirit — this is her story.

SISTER KATE

NURSING THROUGH THE TROUBLES

KATE O'HANLON

LARGE
PRINT

First published in Great Britain 2010
by
Blackstaff Press

First Isis Edition
published 2017
by arrangement with
Blackstaff Press

A catalogue record for this book is available
from the British Library.

ISBN 978–1–78541–404–6 (hb)
ISBN 978–1–78541–410–7 (pb)

Published by
F. A. Thorpe (Publishing)
Anstey, Leicestershire

Set by Words & Graphics Ltd.
Anstey, Leicestershire
Printed and bound in Great Britain by
T. J. International Ltd., Padstow, Cornwall

This book is printed on acid-free paper

Parkhead Library
64 Tollcross Road
Glasgow G31 4XA
Phone: 0141 276 1530

This book is due for return on or before the last date shown below. It may be renewed by telephone, personal application, fax or post, quoting this date, author, title and the book number.

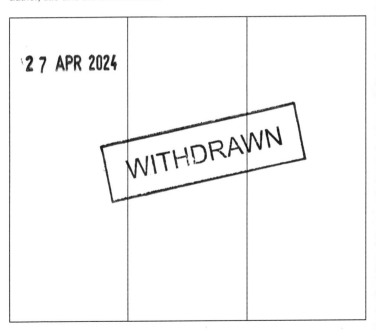

27 APR 2024

WITHDRAWN

To my family

Contents

Born and bred in the Markets

I was born in 1930 in Annette Street, in the Markets district of central Belfast. Some time ago my brother John and I walked round that area, admiring the modern houses. We could not find Annette Street and when we asked a passer-by where it was, he told us that there was no such street. Not only had number 51 disappeared but the whole street had been demolished to make way for the new development. So there is not going be a plaque outside the house where I was born saying "Kate O'Hanlon was born here".

My father's parents were from Omeath, a village in County Louth. His mother and her two sisters went to Boston when she was eighteen. She had been courting my grandfather, who lived a few fields away, and he followed her out. They were married in Chelsea, a Boston suburb, and my father and aunt were born there. In due course, however, the whole family returned to Omeath. During the First World War, my father was living in Liverpool with an aunt. Her two sons, aged nineteen and twenty, were conscripted and killed in action in 1917, but as a United States citizen, my father was able to avoid conscription.

My mother's grandfather and Uncle Pat, who drowned near the pier in 1921, were fishermen in Buncrana in County Donegal. Her father was one of the many Donegal people who travelled to Scotland for seasonal work. He worked on the railways as a labourer, but died of typhoid when he was just twenty-four, and is buried in Greenock in Scotland. My grandmother was with him when he died — she would only have been about twenty-three at the time. My grandmother later emigrated to America, leaving her children behind: her daughter, my mother, aged four, with her maternal family; and her son, Barney, aged two, with his father's people.

My mother grew up in Buncrana, raised by her mother's parents, and spoiled by her doting uncles and aunts. Uncle Barney was reared on a farm and didn't have anywhere near such an easy time. He emigrated to the USA when he was about seventeen years old, much to his grandmother's distress — her weeping on the day he left was so loud that he remembers hearing it right until the end of the road. The only time brother and sister slept under the same roof — that they could remember — was when my mother visited Uncle Barney in America, by which time they both had grown-up families of their own.

My father and mother met in Buncrana and married in 1929 in Kildare town, where my mother was living with an aunt and uncle. Mother was twenty-eight and Father ten years older. For the first six months of their marriage, they lived in the Lough Swilly Hotel in Buncrana — my mother knew the owners of the hotel

2

and my father was working as a fish buyer in the town. They then moved up to Annette Street in the Markets area of Belfast. I was born there the following year; then came my four brothers, George, John, Brian and Patrick. So I was the eldest of five children, and the only girl. My parents had a very happy marriage, and my father used to give us all a kiss as he left for work in the morning, which was very unusual in those days.

There was a mixture of houses in the Markets. Lots were small kitchen houses but we lived in one of the parlour houses — a house with a front room — and there was a large attic room where we kept our toys and played in bad weather. My father was manager in Owen O'Hagan's Wholesale Fish Merchants in the Fish Market in Oxford Street. My mother usually had a girl from the locality or from the country to help with the housework and the children. Not all these girls were entirely happy in their work, however — one was so fond of the work that she sent herself a telegram, saying her mother was sick and she had to go home. The Markets was a great place to live — very close-knit, everybody knew everybody else.

There was a public house at each end of our street, Hans Savage's and Campbell's. When John and I visited the Markets that day, everyone we spoke to so small you had to stoop to get into some of them, and a bathroom where you had to climb steps to get into the bath. The usual way into the house was via the main door that opened onto Hamilton Street, but, as kids, we loved to go in through the hidden door in the bar's storeroom. The bar was a very noisy place, especially at night. Even after closing time people would linger at the street corner, talking for hours on end. I remember my aunt saying that she could never sleep when she went up to Omeath because it was so quiet.

There were some great characters in the area, including well-known boxers and snooker players. A legendary hard man was Silver McKee. A big, good-looking man, Silver took on all-comers and people travelled from all over Ireland to fight him. There are many stories about him. He worked at Allam's Cattle Market, and according to one tale, he rescued a heifer from the Lagan, bringing it ashore. He could be a handful and was banned from Uncle Barney's, but he told me years later that when he got into trouble, my uncle always hired a solicitor for him and paid any fees. Silver was such a likeable rogue that I think Uncle Barney must have had a soft spot for him. I remember sitting in the Royal's casualty reception one day, many years later, enjoying a chat with Silver and three other people from the Markets. Staff passing by thought we looked very clannish. We took it as a compliment, and it reminded us of all the good neighbours we had when we lived there.

Father Dean from St Malachy's church, on Alfred Street, was a well-loved figure, sure to be at all the local sporting fixtures and entertainments. I was baptised, made my first communion and was confirmed at St Malachy's. I attended Sussex Place Convent School for Young Ladies — at least that's what it said on the sign above the front door until quite recently — and to get there I had to walk through Cromac Square, past the well-known bicycle shop, Stone's. I remember very well two of the nuns who taught there: Sister Pius, who was very quiet and gentle, and Sister Cecilia the music teacher. It was Sister Cecilia who told me I had no ear for music. I have often thought that it is no wonder that a lot of Catholics do not sing well in church when the nuns were so discouraging to the young ones.

The Empire Theatre was near our school, a lovely, small theatre in which famous artistes appeared and plays premièred, including some controversial ones. *Over the Bridge*, for example, Sam Thompson's play about sectarianism in the shipyards, had its first performance there many years later. As there were hardly any hotels in those days, the performers — even Charlie Chaplin — stayed in theatrical digs in nearby Joy Street. There were pantomimes every year and the child performers had to go to school, so we had Little Red Riding Hood and the Babes in the Wood sitting beside us in our class for the duration. I even performed at the Empire myself. I was attending May King's tap-dancing class in King Street and performed with the class at the theatre. I can still remember the smell of the greasepaint in the dressing rooms.

Newington Avenue and
further afield

When I was eight, we moved to Newington Avenue, off the Antrim Road in the north side of the city, where my youngest two brothers were born. This was to be my home for many years, in fact until a knee operation in 2000 meant that I could no longer manage the stairs. I was sent to the local school for a short time, which had lay teachers, but then went back to the nuns, this time in the Crumlin Road convent, near the prison. I was attending the convent when nineteen-year-old Tom Williams was hanged at the prison in 1942. I think we must have been given the day off school, because of its proximity to the prison. The young IRA volunteer was buried there until 2000 (the prison closed in 1996), when his remains were exhumed and reburied at Milltown cemetery.

During the Second World War, Belfast was bombed by the Luftwaffe. North Belfast was badly hit in the first German air raid, on Easter Tuesday, April 1941. I remember lying under the table in the living room, feeling very afraid, while some of the family crouched in the coal hole under the stairs. We had a narrow escape when an incendiary device landed on the house next door but failed to explode. One bomb dropped on an air-raid shelter in nearby Atlantic Avenue, and everyone inside was killed.

There were rumours later that the Germans had mistaken the Belfast Waterworks, not far from where we lived, for the docks, and that was why our area, mostly residential, received the full force of the attack. In the city that night, around 900 people were killed and a great many were seriously injured. Hospitals were overwhelmed, especially the Mater Hospital on the Crumlin Road; in the Royal alone 120 casualties were admitted and another 113 were seen and discharged. Bodies were laid out for identification in makeshift morgues in the Falls Road Public Baths and St George's Market.

There were fears of another attack and people panicked, leaving the city in huge numbers — some to the countryside, others to the neutral South. We were among those who went across the border. My mother and us children left for Buncrana and my father joined us at weekends. We went to my mother's aunt, Anne, who was a very gentle, holy woman. My grumpy uncle Frank was a different kettle of fish — my mother had an awful time keeping the five of us quiet enough to please him. We went to school there and everything was taught through Irish. As none of us had a word of Irish except for some prayers, I do not think we could have learned very much. Buncrana was a boom town during the war. Nearby Derry, on the other side of the border, was an important port for the Allies, and many of the soldiers based there — including the Americans — came to Buncrana for recreation. My mother was on the Main Street one day when Prince Philip got out of a car beside her.

The people of Belfast had been right to worry about another attack — it came the following month on 4–5 May. This time the German pilots did not miss the docks and shipyard, but many bombs also fell on commercial and residential areas of the city, especially in east Belfast, and again there were many casualties.

We left Buncrana and went to my father's family home in Omeath. It did not suit my mother, however; I don't think she was ever fond of Omeath, especially at that time when there was no electricity, no running water and a big black range in the kitchen that smoked so badly we often had to run out into the field for a breath of fresh air. Living there was great fun for us children, however, and for all the family who came to visit for their holidays. Adults slept in the beds and the children slept on the floor. I do not know how my mother looked after us all. Every Saturday we watched for Daddy coming up from the bus-stop on the lower road and ran down through the fields to meet him. I am sure my mother was worried sick about his safety when he was in the city.

The boys went to school in Omeath but I was sent to a boarding school run by the Mercy nuns in Newry, and stayed there even when the rest of the family moved back to Belfast. I was too young for the big school and was placed in the kindergarten with a few other children; a governess, Miss Gordon, looked after us. We were never allowed to join in the games or go on cinema trips or do anything enjoyable with the big girls. I hated it and cried to be taken home each time I had a visitor. The nuns threatened to stop all visits unless I behaved myself.

My lucky day was when I got scarlet fever. I was bundled into a taxi and taken to Daisy Hill Hospital. In all, eight pupils were admitted to the hospital with the illness and the school was closed. There was no segregation in the wards, with diphtheria in one bed and scarlet fever next door. When we were on our feet, we helped with the meals in all the wards. I must have been in hospital for about two weeks. Two days after I arrived home two of my brothers got diphtheria and were taken off in a darkened ambulance to Purdysburn Hospital. They were very ill; I had carried the diphtheria home.

I never went back to the boarding school, for which I was very thankful. Instead, I returned to the Crumlin Road convent, and later won a city scholarship which enabled me to go to any grammar school in Belfast I wanted. The scholarship covered board, books — everything really. I chose to go to the Dominican College in Fortwilliam Park where I was very happy.

Around the time I turned fourteen, in November 1944, I was out walking with my father. I said to him that now I was of an age when I could go to work. He looked at me and said nothing, which meant that he had no intention of letting me leave school. However he died the following April, when he was just fifty-four, and my mother was left with the five of us. We had very little money, just the widow's pension and family allowance — if one went up, she always said, the other was guaranteed to go down.

I left school and went to work in my father's old office, Owen O'Hagan's, at the Fish Market, attending night classes and obtaining qualifications in book-keeping, shorthand, typing and English. During those years, when I wasn't working, studying or at night classes, I was helping to run a youth club in Lonsdale Street, off the Crumlin Road. I'd become involved through joining the Legion of Mary in St Patrick's Parish, Donegall Street. Lonsdale Street, which doesn't exist now, was once a beautiful road of big houses owned by wealthy families, but in the 1950s had become much more downmarket, with only four houses still occupied by single families, and the rest with a family in every room — each kitchen, each parlour, each bedroom — and only one toilet. The Mater Hospital owned the big house at the top of the street. It was let to the Young Men's Christian Association and they allowed us to use the top two rooms for the youth club. About sixty children came to the club most nights of the week and we taught them singing, dancing and games, and put on concerts and pantomimes. I also ran netball teams — I was already playing for the Fortwilliam Past Pupils second team — and we practised on waste ground that occupied about two thirds of the left-hand side of the street.

The nurses who lived in the Mater's nurses' home, opposite Lonsdale Street, used to have great fun watching the girls from the two Lonsdale Street brothels standing on the corner, and the cars that came to pick them up. It was 1951 and government census takers were not welcome in many of the houses on the street, so they asked us to take the details for them. We could go anywhere we wanted as we were looking after the local children. We couldn't believe the numbers of people living, eating and sleeping in a single room.

One weekend, five of us took sixty of the children to the Drumalis retreat centre in Larne. Most of them had never been on a train or left Belfast before. I can't honestly say that their behaviour was the best, and the nuns said that they could never come back. Father Arthurs from Clonard was the priest leading the retreat and he firmly felt it was all worthwhile, in spite of the children's high spirits. This was because a twelve-year-old girl had confided in him about a problem she was having — she'd never felt able to talk to anyone else about it — and he was able to help her.

I also joined the ambulance corps of the Order of Malta (which is short for the Sovereign Military Hospitaller Order of Saint John of Jerusalem, of Rhodes, and of Malta) and was trained in First Aid. The corps covered sporting events, cinemas, theatres and church services. We also learned home nursing and were examined by a sister from the Mater. She was a very tough lady.

Years later, when I was working at the Royal, two other nurses and I started a home nursing course for the Order of Malta. The Mater Hospital kindly allowed us to use their Day Procedure Unit for the practical part of the course. In the beginning, many of the students who came on the course had sick relatives whom they wanted to care for at home, but in later years people took the course in order to get jobs as carers and auxiliaries. We also put some of the students who had successfully completed the course on to the wards of the Mater as volunteers. They were supervised and had to adhere to strict protocols. Over the years, though, the numbers fell, in spite of advertising, and with just four on the course one year, we decided to stop the courses. I always hoped that I was easier on my students than the sister at the Mater had been on us all those years ago.

After I'd worked in the office for twelve years I was ready for a change and a new challenge. Nursing seemed like the best career option open to me at the time. My brothers had chosen their professions too — George was ordained as a priest in 1957; John was a teacher; Brian was a quantity surveyor; and Patrick was at teacher training college.

Nurse training at the Royal

Today, most universities offering degrees in nursing require students to have at least three A levels at good grades. When I applied to begin training in the Royal Victoria Hospital I had to sit an entrance examination, consisting of mathematics and English, which I passed, and I had an interview with the matron, Florence Elliott (Miss Elliott to us), and Lady Johnston of the management committee. I imagine they thought an old lady like me would not be able to finish the course. My name was put on the waiting list nevertheless, and eighteen months later, in 1958, at the grand old age of twenty-seven, I started my nurse training.

First I went to the Beeches, Hampton Park, at the top of the Ormeau Road in south Belfast, a lovely old house standing in its own grounds. There were twenty-three of us and we were very lucky to be together for three months, studying, working in the wards, supporting each other. Nurses today miss so much of the support and comradeship we enjoyed.

We had lectures and practical training at the Beeches. Tutors taught us basic anatomy and physiology, and practical skills such as changing beds and washing patients.

After two weeks, we spent one day each week at the hospital, under the supervision of a senior nurse or staff nurse. I remember the smell of the hospital, the heat, the constant sore feet. The uniforms were cumbersome — stiff white collars with studs, and stiff belts; and dress hemlines at mid-calf. I did not feel like a little "angel", or even like a big one. I was terrified if a patient asked me to do anything.

Matron came to visit us in the Beeches in our first week. "Where are my Catholic nurses?" she asked. Noeleen McGovern and I put up our hands. We thought we were getting a special welcome — at least everyone now knew who we were. No other hands went up, so out of an intake of twenty-three, only two of us were Catholic. The Royal had a reputation for being a Protestant hospital, and the powers that be had apparently decided to have two Catholics to keep one another company, so that we would not mix with the others. We were a very mixed crowd. I was by far the eldest; most were just eighteen years old, straight out of school. Naturally, cliques formed. Five of us became close friends: Noeleen, Betty Monaghan, Edna Malcolmson, Daphne Carson and me, and there was never a trace of sectarian behaviour or discrimination among us. It was a happy time.

Having come through the initial training, we moved to the Royal and were allocated accommodation in the West Wing of the hospital. These rooms are now the offices of the cardiology department. They were very basic and cold, with big bathrooms on every corridor. An assistant matron in the dining room in the wing served meals. Nurses ate alone. We had to be in by ten thirty every night. There was very little chance of disobeying this rule, as the only entrance to the wing was down the main corridor, open to the world with no hiding place. One late pass per week was allowed. Imagine today's nurses standing for that. Of course, there were unofficial ways to get in, as there always will be in a nurses' home. At twenty-seven, however, I was too exhausted after a day on the wards to care, but some of the younger ones found the set-up more restrictive. Miss Duff was in charge of the nurses' living quarters. She checked the bedrooms every morning to make sure that everything was tidy. Very strict, she once fetched a friend of mine who had not had time to make her bed back from the ward to do it.

In a seven-day working week we had one full day plus one half day off, when we could go home. The shifts were long: we started on the wards at 7a.m. and returned to West Wing around 8.30 or 9 for breakfast. Then we finished for the day at 5.30p.m., or worked until 1p.m., returning at 4.30p.m. to go through until 8.30p.m. On Sundays we either worked from 7a.m. until 2p.m. or from 2p.m. until 9p.m. Our feet would be sore and swollen, and we used to prop up one end of our beds with books so that our feet were raised when we slept.

I made firm friends in those early days, and without their humour and support life would have been very difficult, especially when we were on nights: six nights on duty and three nights off for three months, working from 8p.m. until 7.30a.m. For our night duty in first year we stayed in Lennoxvale, another beautiful, big house, on the Malone Road — the wealthy end of town. The house itself was very cold, but the food was excellent, cooked on the premises. When we came off duty, we caught taxis from the Royal back to Lennoxvale, then made a dash to avoid being last in the queue for water for our hot-water bottles. For meals at the hospital we each had our own seat in the dining room, allocated according to which ward we were in, and we sat in order of seniority. Green badges for first year, blue badges for second year and red badges for third year. Night sister could see at a glance who was absent from meals.

Miss Elliott and the assistant matrons paid out our salary in Matron's office. There was great checking of uniforms and shoes outside in the queue; if you were not perfectly turned out, you did not get your wages and had to go back to your room and change. We received the grand sum of £9 a month. In those days, money was a dirty word in the world of nursing, and certainly not something that trainees like us would mention. We were content with our pay and dedicated to our chosen career. Looking back, I think we were all a bit naïve. We were members of the Royal College of Nursing (RCN), a good professional body, but by no means a trade union. When male nurses entered the profession the situation began to change. Some were married, with families and mortgages, and they demanded fair pay. Wanting to reach the top quickly, they worked hard and stood up for nurses' rights.

On Sunday mornings Noeleen and I went to early morning Mass at six o'clock in Clonard Monastery on the Falls Road. We had to go in uniform, as we went on duty immediately afterwards. Going out in uniform was not allowed, however, and one particular night sister was always waiting to reprimand us when we arrived at the hospital. The only time the rule about wearing uniform outside was relaxed was during the Troubles, when we were occasionally allowed to travel in uniform for safety. Later, Mass was celebrated at 5p.m. for hospital staff at St Malachy's, Alfred Street. At the Royal today there are three Masses on Sundays for patients and staff.

It was a shock to the system going on the wards for the first time, wearing my green badge. We could not show embarrassment or lack of confidence as the patients almost certainly felt much worse than we did. My first ward was medical unit 7/8, and like all the wards on the main corridor, it was a Nightingale ward — a large open-plan dormitory ward, as opposed to the wards made up of four to six bed bays that are more common today. Some patients today say that they preferred the old Nightingale wards to the new four-or six-bed bays: they felt safer and liked that they were able to see a nurse from their bed. The downside was the lack of privacy. The two consultants on medical unit 7/8 were Terence Fulton and John Weaver, both great gentlemen. I remember the surprise I felt one day when Dr Fulton opened a door for me — certainly not the way we student nurses expected to be treated by consultants.

Each ward had a sister in charge, who wore a red uniform and was responsible for overseeing the ward and all administration; a junior sister in a navy blue uniform, whose job it was to teach and supervise nurses; and qualified staff nurses who, if good at their jobs, would give student nurses the chance to see more of the complex nursing jobs. Usually about three student nurses worked on a ward, and our main responsibility was the care and comfort of the patient, and looking after the relatives. We also performed a lot of non-nursing duties. There was no sterile supply department, so the drums had to be packed with dressings on the ward and taken to the steriliser. If Matron came in while you were packing a drum, she would tell you to sit down, a rare moment in a ward. We also sterilised instruments and equipment in the sterilisers in the wards.

The wards in those days were strictly run, not least because everyone, including some consultants, was in awe of the sister in charge. First-years did not address senior staff, and certainly not the doctors; there was a definite chain of command. Not all of our seniors were pleasant and kind; there were a few real bullies. I never minded constructive criticism, and it was a good feeling to be thanked by the sister or staff nurse for a task well done or for working hard on a busy day. When I became a sister, I always tried to remember to thank the nurses for their work.

During our training we had to work in medical and surgical wards; gynaecology; some of the specialities, such as neurosurgery; and either Purdysburn Psychiatric

Hospital, the psychiatric hospital for the Greater Belfast area, or the Royal Belfast Hospital for Sick Children. I worked for one month in Graham Clinic, the admission and observation ward at Purdysburn. Now called Knockbracken Healthcare Park, it is a large estate on the outskirts of south Belfast. Units, called villas, are dotted throughout the grounds, each with its own security arrangements, and treating different conditions. Buses transported staff and patients around the grounds, from the villas to the canteens, to church, and so on.

I found it a very different experience working in a psychiatric hospital. Apart from learning about psychiatric problems, I learned to observe people and listen closely. In general nursing, if we sat down to talk and listen to patients, we would feel guilty, knowing that many other things were crying out to be done. We would probably receive a lecture from the sister into the bargain, even though listening and talking to patients undoubtedly is an important part of nursing. If there was little time for this in my day, it seems that today there is no time at all for talking to anyone or listening to patients' problems. There are not enough nurses to do the basic nursing tasks, never mind giving psychological support.

Back at the Royal we went to Musson House for lectures and practical training one day a week. These sessions covered surgical, medical, neurosurgical, burns and orthopaedic nursing, as well as dietetics and pharmacology. I nursed in the fracture ward. The Japanese motorcycling champion Kenji Tanaka came in from Dundrod, injured from an accident at the Ulster Grand Prix. His legs were fractured and there was some concern they would have to be amputated. He had been wearing very short boots and all the dirt of Dundrod was in his wounds. The man in the next bed, Walter, had been a soldier in the Far East and his family brought food and gifts to Kenji. Whatever Walter got, Kenji got too. He did not speak English but he quickly learned a few words from the other men, mostly rude. He may not have known what he was saying exactly, but he knew well enough that it was not good. Showing embarrassment in this ward was a bad idea. It was full of young, healthy men, usually with broken limbs from motorcycle accidents, and they were bored and raring to get into mischief. The nurses were the obvious targets. Eventually, a Japanese doctor came to bring Kenji home, and with physiotherapy and good care his legs were saved.

It was the custom not to send first-year nurses to the neurosurgical unit, but I spent the last three months of my first year there. The work was very hard and caring for so many young people who were paralysed affected me deeply. Although there was great support in this unit from the sisters, senior nurses and doctors, in my short spell there I could not get used it and was glad to leave.

I went back to the unit again in my second year, however, on night duty. I spent all my time "specialling" very ill patients — that is, one-to-one nursing around the clock. We had no intensive care unit at that time. One night I was with a man who had been injured in the shipyard. He was not going to get better. I told Dr Bob Gray, the anaesthetist, that I could not take much more of this, as this patient would be the sixth who had died while I was caring for them. Dr Gray said, "Never mind, my face is the last face most patients see before they see St Peter." He was a kind man and friendly to everyone, and always had a joke. When I worked in the casualty department after I qualified, it was a pleasure to see him visit the seriously ill patients. He was calm and efficient and I knew the patient was going to receive the best of care. The intensive care unit was very fortunate to have him as their consultant when it opened in later years.

In the neurosurgical unit we frequently had to keep special patients in hypothermia, nursing them in ice to keep their temperature down. The patient was packed in ice, the windows were thrown wide open and a fan wafted the cold air about the room. We nurses wore as many clothes as possible beneath our white gowns; we even wore gloves. Looking back, it seems a wonder that the nurses themselves survived, but I never got so much as a cold.

I specialled a young boy for ten nights. He had been a bright boy, then had a personality change, becoming aggressive. It turned out that he had a brain tumour. His family brought over a professor from Scotland, but unfortunately nothing could be done for him by this professor or the Royal's excellent neurosurgeons. We tried everything: nursing in ice, oxygen tent, respirator, but all in vain, and he died early one morning before I came off duty. The nurse in charge, Sheila Payne, later came to my room in Mussen House. She stayed and talked to me for some time. I have never forgotten her kindness.

Despite my initial feelings about this unit, I had come to love working there, and in my third year I went back on night duty as nurse in charge — an arrangement that would not be allowed today; now a staff nurse is always in charge of neurosurgery. We rarely got a chance to sit down; staff in other wards would put out the chairs and have some rest during the night, but not us. Neurosurgical emergencies came from all over the country and at all hours. In a night emergency, we got the theatre ready and assisted until the regular theatre staff arrived from home. I remember a boy rushed from the country straight to theatre but there was no hope for him. He had been hit on the head by a hockey ball. His parents were with him; their only son. He died just before we went off duty.

A young woman was brought in one Easter. She had been involved in a road accident and was paralysed from the neck down. The first day we lifted her out of bed she fainted from the shock, but after that she got used to being lifted out every day. She was very attractive and obviously had enjoyed a full social life. She was a good patient, a bit spoiled, perhaps, with all the attention both inside and outside the hospital. That is, if you can call anyone who cannot move, spoiled. Some celebrities came over from England and presented her with a television set. She loved to have her nails manicured and hair properly done, and we would put on her make-up for her, and spray her with

22

Worth perfume. She received a good insurance settlement but no amount of money could ever compensate her for the loss of her freedom. Thirty years later, I heard a message played on the radio for her, mentioning that she was in a nursing home. Apparently she was still only able to move a finger but managed to stay in good form — she had great spirit.

My friend Betty looked after the nursery on night duty in the unit. There were usually about six babies needing care, suffering from spina bifida, hydrocephalus and tumours. Betty was a perfectionist in nursing and those babies were well looked after. Every morning they would be dressed beautifully. Betty had the highest standards.

On Christmas Day, all units had a full complement of staff. Patients who were fit enough went home for the day, so we really only had the very ill ones to look after. On my first Christmas I specialled a young woman who was unconscious from a drug overdose. I was with her nearly all day and missed some of the Christmas entertainment. Traditionally, nurses were allowed to visit the other wards, which were decorated for the occasion, each with its own Christmas tree. A hospital fund paid for Christmas presents for the patients and helped with the cost of decorations and festive fare. The day would start with a choir comprised of hospital staff going round all the wards singing carols, accompanied by a piano-player pushed on a trolley. Santa Claus was next, not many presents though, just a bit of a carry-on. The turkeys were roasted in the hospital kitchens and there was quite a ceremony in each ward, with consultants in charge of the carving and serving the patients. The consultants' families would arrive in the morning and a party went on all day in one of the side wards. At night most of the staff sat down to a proper meal and a bit of fun. Years later, when I was working in the casualty department, the decorations were stolen from our tree on Level 3. I put up a notice explaining why the tree was bare. The next day it was covered with decorations again — everyone passing had brought one in.

I qualified in 1961, and from May to November I was staff nurse in the professorial surgical unit, ward 12, one of the busiest wards in the hospital. The months after you qualify, when you are staffing in your hospital, are the best of your nursing career. One day you are a student nurse and the next you have to accept the responsibilities of a staff nurse, which means being in charge when the sister is off duty. How much more difficult it is for nurses today. When they qualify, they have spent very little time with patients, and have not performed the basic tasks we took so much for granted. Jean McAllister, nearly one year ahead of me, was the staff nurse in ward 11. She was a great help, and whenever I was in any difficulty, I would ask her advice. I was very happy in this unit and learned a great deal. But when the year came to an end, it was time to leave for my midwifery training.

Midwifery at Liverpool and back home

Almost every nurse, once she qualified, stayed six to nine months in the Royal. There was then the option to do a course in midwifery, which you needed if you wanted to become a sister. Today midwifery is an optional part of the general nursing course, and there are additional courses in Accident & Emergency, Intensive Care, and Theatre. In my view, however, you are not a nurse, in the full sense of the word, unless you can deliver a baby. Miss Elliott encouraged all of us to go to England or Scotland for this training — she felt that going to the Royal Maternity was "just going over the grass", which of course it was, since the maternity hospital is situated in the grounds close to the main hospital. One shy country girl was encouraged to go to London. She had never been out of Northern Ireland and she went to London on her own. I never heard what became of her, but the experience will either have killed her or cured her. I picked Liverpool because my aunt and uncle lived there and the maternity hospital was very modern and had a good reputation. Professor

Coates worked there; the book he wrote was a standard reference in maternity hospitals in the United Kingdom.

Auntie Minnie, my father's sister, and Uncle Larry had owned a fruit shop in east Belfast but were burned out during one of the pogroms in the 1920s. They moved to Bootle in north Liverpool, an area that reminded me of the Markets — very close-knit, with everyone helpful and friendly. All relatives who landed in England would beat a path to Minnie and Larry's door in Chaucer Street and were sure of the warmest welcome.

I was the only Irish nurse in the group of nine that started at Liverpool Maternity Hospital. We made friends quickly and went everywhere together when we were off duty. The Empire and Playhouse theatres supplied nurses with front-row passes and we saw all the musicals before they went to the West End. We got stand tickets to see Liverpool playing at Anfield from one of the club's directors, whose baby we had delivered. And one rainy day we went to the Grand National at Aintree. We stood too near one of the jumps and as the horses flew past the mud spattered up round us and ruined our clothes. We managed to back the winner in the first race, so all was not lost.

Although I enjoyed my time in Liverpool, I still came home to Belfast as often as I could. The airfare was only eight pounds, but the plane took longer than it needed to as it always stopped in the Isle of Man.

We had a lot of studying to do in Liverpool and we worked very hard in the wards. We gained lots of experience in the outpatient and antenatal clinics, the antenatal and postnatal wards, and the labour wards. At my first birth I had a sense of awe, I felt that I was witnessing a miracle, and even after many deliveries this feeling never left me. In those days there were no intensive care units for premature babies; they were nursed in the same ward as their mothers. We had to prepare all the feeds, feed the babies during the night, and encourage and supervise the breastfeeding mothers. It seems to me that we had more time to spend with mothers than midwives today. Mostly these were happy times, but there were some sorrowful moments when babies were born dead or so deformed as to be incompatible with life.

Our nurses' home consisted of three houses. To reach them, we had to walk through a square, surrounded on all four sides by university buildings which were closed at night. These buildings bordered the red light district and some disreputable clubs. At night we went home in pairs or in a group, as we were propositioned regularly. We soon learned there was a fortune to be made in Liverpool and it was not from nursing. We could have made more money in one night in that trade than we made in a whole year as pupil midwives.

In those days, many people had their babies at home, delivered by district midwives. There was always a maternity ambulance available that we could call in case of emergency, but I did not have to call it out during my six months on district in Liverpool. During that time, we lived in a big house in Norwood Grove, and we took it in turn to be on call at night. Visits were made by bicycle or bus, and for deliveries we took taxis. I enjoyed delivering babies in their homes; you felt part of the family, with Granny, the children and sometimes Father present. There'd be frequent cups of tea, and if it was a long labour, a big fry might be served up to keep you going.

I qualified as a midwife and returned to the Royal in 1963. I was put in temporary charge of wards 23 and 24, the gynaecological unit. Sister Kathleen Galbraith, who was usually in charge of that ward, was on holiday, and her deputy, Sister Lilias Wallace, was ill — in fact she was a patient in the hospital. At that time I was thinking about working abroad. To work in America I needed psychiatric and paediatric experience, so I returned to Purdysburn for three months. We are all supposed to remember where we were when we heard about the assassination of John F. Kennedy. Well, I was calling bingo in Rathlin villa at Purdysburn. My spell there was productive, if not always happy. I found it depressing to see young, discharged patients being readmitted during my short time there.

The Royal Belfast Hospital for Sick Children was my next port of call. I quickly found that paediatric nursing was not for me: it requires a different kind of nurse and great patience. In my experience, paediatric nurses have a vocation, not just for nursing, but for working with children and babies too. And so I returned to the Royal, and Miss Elliott said, "Welcome home".

The old casualty department

I ended up in the casualty department, in charge on night duty, as a result of an administrative mistake. I had not worked in the department before. I had worked for a while in outpatients, so it was assumed that I had worked in casualty — they were all in the same block. Real experience is needed to take charge of casualty, however, and since I had no experience at all, I relied heavily on the part-time nurses who had worked there for years.

I had not worked there for long when my mother died. One night, in April 1964, after I had come home from casualty, my mother went upstairs. We heard her cry out for my youngest brother, Paddy, and when we ran up to her, she was complaining of severe chest pain and looked shocked. We carried her up the three stairs to her room and put her in bed, clothes and all. Dr McNeill, the family GP, came shortly after, and said she had had a massive heart attack and could not be moved to the hospital. How things have changed for the better since then — no cardiac ambulance in those days. She gave Mammy morphia, and left more with me to give as required. We called Father Breen from

29

Holy Family, our local church on the Limestone Road, and he was a great support, ringing other family members, including my brother George, who at that time was a curate in Portaferry. We also contacted my brother Brian in London and my aunt. My brothers John and George arrived, and we sat and watched, prayed and talked. George prayed with Mammy and us. She became restless and there was more pain. I phoned Dr McNeill and she said, "You must know what will happen, there is nothing more we can do." I gave her another morphine injection and she settled a bit.

Someone was holding her hands as we were saying the Rosary and the prayers for the dying, and she died quietly and without a sound. She had been at 7 o'clock Mass the morning before she died, as she was every day. After she was dressed in her shroud, her hands were bound with the cord that had been part of my brother's vestments on his ordination day. Fr Breen phoned to enquire about her, and he said he would have her prayed for at the 7 o'clock Mass. The congregation was shocked and the first callers arrived at the house after Mass. I wished some of her close friends had heard the news of her death from me rather than hearing in public, at church. There was a constant stream of visitors until the following evening when her body was brought to the church. We did not know half the people who called but my mother always spoke to everyone and seemed to know the entire parish.

My brother's fellow priests called, and relatives started to arrive. We sent a telegram to America, where Mammy's brother and his extended family lived. My mother had been in Boston the previous year, and it was the first time she and her brother had spent time together since they were children. Her death would not have been so hard on him and his family if they had not known her. They phoned up during the early hours of the morning — they thought we were having an old Irish wake and staying up all night. The chapel was packed for the funeral. I was sitting between Auntie Bee, a relation by marriage and a close family friend, and my mother's cousin Anthony from Buncrana. When we saw the Bishop coming out on the altar, we whispered to each other that Mammy would be pleased to see this. She always used to say, "When I go I will have a big funeral". She also said, "When you are all reared I am going," and she did.

I never cried at the funeral or in the subsequent days. Some thought it was part of my training but in fact I was too shocked at the suddenness of her death. When I went back to work a week later and saw stroke patients and others suffering with cancer, I tried to thank God for my mother's mercifully quick death at home, surrounded by her family. Many months later I had abdominal pain. The doctors thought it was caused by an ulcer but tests showed there was nothing wrong with me. There is an old Chinese proverb that goes: "If the eye does not weep, the gut will." I believe that is what happened to me.

I was very touched when Joan and Maureen, two of my friends from Liverpool, offered to come over and Miss Elliott was also very kind to me at that time. She was a great matron — very strict, of course, but just.

She was Matron at the Royal for twenty years, from 1946 to 1966. I remember during my student days passing her on the corridor with my hands in my bib. As she slowly walked by she said: "I do not like to see my nurses with their hands in their bibs." I never did it again. When I returned to work after Mammy died, I was thinking of doing district midwifery because I thought it would be easier to look after my home and my two brothers who shared it with me if I were working on the district. I went to talk to Miss Elliott about it. She phoned the nurse in charge of community services. I was interviewed and subsequently set up at home with a plate outside the front door, saying Kathleen O'Hanlon, SCN (State Registered Nurse), SCM (State Certified Midwife).

As a district midwife, I visited the homes of mothers before the birth to make sure they were clean and well enough equipped, delivered the babies, and visited after the birth. I remember one delivery in particular, the sixth child in the family, at a house near the docks. All went well. When I visited the next day, I was surprised to see the infant was having Farex baby food, a kind of gruel, when he certainly shouldn't have been having anything but milk. I thought to myself, this woman has had five children, who am I to say anything to her? So I said nothing. As I was leaving I met her GP, a great maternity doctor, coming up the stairs. I told him about the Farex and he too decided to say nothing.

The work was enjoyable, but there was a problem. Many women were now opting to have their babies in hospital and, as a result, there was a decline in home

32

deliveries. So I was not very busy. I spent most of my time at home waiting for phone calls, doing clinics with the local GPs and covering other midwives when they were off duty. It would have been the ideal job for a married woman with family responsibilities, but I was getting bored. After a year I resigned. Miss Baird, who was in charge of district nurses and midwives on behalf of Belfast City Council, remarked that I was the first nurse to leave because there was not enough work. I did not give up midwifery immediately but joined the Malone Place General Practitioners Unit, which was run by midwives for the GPs. The patients were mostly nurses, doctors' wives and doctors. Midwives delivered most of the babies. A doctor was required to be present for at least part of the time but all the midwives were very experienced and any emergencies were sent to the nearby Jubilee Hospital, which was in the grounds of the City Hospital on the Lisburn Road.

One of my friends who was a midwife — a lovely, quiet, very efficient woman — was also a fervent wrestling fan. We all went along to the fights in the Ulster Hall with her, mostly to enjoy the antics of our friend. It was a laugh sitting in the front row, overlooking the ring and watching the punters rant and rail at the wrestlers, especially our friend, who became a completely different person at these bouts. In her excitement she was nearly over the balcony on a few occasions.

I made good friends in all my midwifery work and still meet mothers whose babies I delivered in Belfast, although my babies are now mothers themselves. I stayed nine months in Malone Place and then ended this part of my career. I returned once more to the Royal, and because I had experience in casualty, I went straight to that department, where I stayed until my retirement in 1988.

Casualty has always been a popular place for nurses to work — they like the variety and the unpredictability of the work. And it is the shop window of the hospital — what casualty staff do and how they behave reflects on the whole establishment. Mary Galbraith was the sister in charge when I joined the unit. We had to count everything in the unit each morning, including bowls and thermometers. Woe betide us if anything was missing. In later years, when I was the sister in charge, I would have liked to have imposed the same practice, since things went missing all the time but the department was too big and busy by then, and we were trying to cope with the start of the Troubles. We would go on duty some mornings in the new department and the very plugs from the lamps beside the trolleys would have disappeared, cut from the cable. It was decided that if anything was stolen, no matter how small, the police would be informed. One morning, a man was caught stealing three bandages. Unfortunately for him he was on probation and was sentenced to a jail term. It was a great insult to his pride to go to jail for three bandages.

The old casualty department was located in what is now the patients' kitchen on the main hospital corridor. Ambulances came in at the Gate Lodge entrance on the Grosvenor Road, which was also the public entrance to the department. The seriously injured who arrived by ambulance were taken to the ambulance room, and the walking wounded went to the reception desk, in the hall leading into the main hospital corridor, where the receptionist asked some questions to gauge their condition. The fracture clinic, transport office, and reception and admission office all neighboured our department. Upstairs were the outpatient clinics and the almoners' (social workers) offices.

We had five small cubicles in the ambulance room, with minimum resuscitation equipment. The cubicles were so narrow that if a number of staff were treating a patient at the same time, it could become very crowded, and occasionally we even blocked each other's exit. More resuscitation equipment was kept outside the sisters' office and in any cupboards that had extra room. Patients waiting to be seen sat on a bench outside this office. Looking back, it is amazing that we managed to work in such cramped conditions. We also had eight other cubicles for patients with minor injuries and for review, and two theatres.

The public toilets were situated opposite our unit and some of our regular customers slept there. Jimmy arrived every morning to wash in the toilets; he sometimes even washed his shirt. He was frequently drunk but never a menace. When we moved to the new department, he brought me a bunch of flowers for Mother's Day, saying he had no mother of his own. He had picked them off a grave in the City Cemetery on his way down the Falls Road to the hospital. Many years later he died in the Royal in the orthopaedic ward from the horrific injuries he received in a road accident.

Maggie was another character, not quite as quiet as Jimmy in drink. She had the most number of convictions for being drunk and disorderly in Northern Ireland. She had great command of the English language, swearing and cursing all the time. Jean Shaw, who was in charge of the patients' guides, and I visited her once in Armagh jail, a bitterly cold place, and all she wanted was the cigarettes we had brought her. We saw many characters with drink problems in casualty, some from stable, caring families and others from less fortunate backgrounds — when it came to alcohol addiction, it seemed people from all walks of life could be equally blighted.

A large waiting area was just outside the department, originally with wooden benches, then chairs, and finally some soft seats. James Young, the well-known Belfast comedian beloved for his hilarious and affectionate satires about both communities in the North, used to sit here on Friday and Saturday nights, closely observing the goings-on, gathering material for his sketches. Years after his death, I was sitting in a traffic jam in Smithfield and a shop was playing one of his tapes. One by one, the pedestrians stopped and listened and laughed, and every driver was smiling.

We treated everyone, from people who had taken drug overdoses and victims of road accidents to inebriated down-and-outs and those suffering from chest pains. We were able to sit down most nights around 2a.m. for a well-earned rest. The only patients after that would be night-shift men from Mackies factory, the nearby engineering firm, or the sergeant from the Springfield Road barracks who regularly called in for "white medicine for his stomach". At 4a.m. we'd go to the Bostock House restaurant, walking back along Mussen Road, up to the lights at the top of the Grosvenor Road and then into the Royal. At around seven, Connie, the domestic, made tea and toast for everyone who had been on night duty.

Miss Hazel Gaw, the night superintendent, could smell cooking — or cigarette smoke — from one end of the hospital to the other, although she never really minded if you had the occasional cup of tea on duty. For twenty-three years she did her nightly rounds, an imposing figure in a navy frock and cap. Like many senior nurses, there was a kind person — and one with a good sense of humour — beneath the stern appearance, but for all that, the nurses were still frightened of her. I think she knew everything going on in the hospital, but as long as you looked after the patients and did not do anything too extreme, she would turn a blind eye. She would sometimes come back to casualty after her early morning round and we would phone the other staff to warn them she was on her way. Passing our desk, knowing our routine, she would say, "Well, have you made your phone call yet?"

Casualty was not a popular place for doctors to work. For them, there was no training programme and little chance of promotion. We had no dedicated A & E consultant when I first worked in the unit; between them, two hospital consultants — Mr Reggie

Livingston and Mr Willoughby Wilson, both general surgeons — looked after us. We had two medical assistants (the grade above senior registrar), and the rest of the medical staff consisted of housemen, just qualified.

In 1968, Mr William Rutherford came to the department as medical assistant. He had worked for a long time in India, where he had been involved in all aspects of medicine, including nursing. Genuinely interested in A & E work, he was a founding member of the Casualty Surgeons Association and later became its president. He campaigned tirelessly for A & E training for doctors and for the appointment of A & E consultants. All these changes took place when we moved to our new building. A & E medicine owes a great deal to him, not only at the Royal but worldwide. We were also very fortunate to have Dr Peter Nelson as our second consultant; he was a brilliant doctor and a great help to all staff. He and Mr Rutherford were co-authors of *Accident & Emergency Medicine*, a textbook in use in every A & E department in the UK. Sadly, Dr Nelson died from cancer at a young age, and the medical profession lost a great physician. Some years later a training scheme was started for doctors leading to a further degree in emergency medicine, and with better prospects of promotion, doctors began to enter the speciality.

A nine-month A & E course started for nurses some years later, and further training in the treatment of trauma victims and resuscitation techniques was introduced. Today, nurse practitioners can treat certain minor ailments without the involvement of a doctor, and a few hospitals have appointed A & E nurse consultants.

By 1965, work on the new nine-storey Outpatient Building was under way at the Royal, and our department was to be moved to Level 2 of this building. The construction went on until 1969. There was a lot of preparation and a lot of talk during the months preceding our move to the new department. We began to feel like a family leaving its old kitchen-house community for better, more spacious accommodation elsewhere — we had no modern amenities but we were a close-knit, supportive group of people and we were concerned that this camaraderie would be lost in the move. But we need not have worried; we were a great team and we brought all our skill, dedication and comradeship to the new department with us. Of course, there was no longer a place for some of our less orthodox practices — like ambulance man John Ferguson's Irish stew, which he served up to us all every Saturday morning, the smell of it deliciously wafting through the main corridor — such things just did not seem fitting in our new, state-of-the-art surroundings.

We made the move in April 1969. It was as though someone had foreseen that the Troubles in Northern Ireland were about to erupt. When the violence broke out in August of that year, we were well equipped in our new, spacious Accident and Emergency department to cope with what was to come, but nothing could have prepared us for the years that followed.

The new A & E department

The move to the new department took two days. We did not take any emergencies over this time: all emergencies were diverted to the other city hospitals. It was a big change — we now had a spacious unit, well designed and with the most modern, up-to-date equipment — and it took a while familiarising ourselves even with the layout of the place. One drawback was the lack of adequate rest rooms for the doctors and nurses and no teaching room had been provided. Otherwise, we were very lucky to have such a large department, especially in view of the influx of emergencies we would be contending with later that year, and for a long time to come.

The geography of our department proved very significant during major disasters. We were on Level 2 of a nine-storey building. The main entrance to the hospital was on the Falls Road, directly into Level 3. There was a large waiting area, which could be used by relatives or the press in the case of a major incident, and behind that was the physiotherapy department, with a large gymnasium, a space that could be utilised as a holding area for patients waiting to go to other hospitals or to go home during a disaster. Folding beds, blankets and pillows were stored for this purpose. Level 5 to Level 9 were the outpatient clinics. Thus, in an emergency we did not have to call for doctors — they heard the ambulances arriving and would make their way quickly to A & E.

Ambulances reached the department by driving down a sloping roadway to our door. On occasion we had army vehicles, taxis and, once, even a bus arriving with casualties. Although a flashing light indicated that an emergency was due to arrive, and the security men tried hard to keep the access clear, there were often traffic jams at this door. As a result, ambulances were frequently unable to get close to the entrance with their casualties, meaning that seriously injured patients had to be wheeled downhill on trolleys. That was bad planning — more space should have been allocated for ambulance access.

Ambulant patients came in another door, went to the reception desk and were directed to the appropriate area. The receptionists occupied two-thirds of the front desk, and the ambulance service the rest. The service dealt with patients requiring transport to the hospital for appointments and with those going back home or to other hospitals. Unfortunately there was a lot of abuse directed at the receptionists, and a glass screen with a talking aperture had to be erected around the desk.

Not long after the move, I was made a sister. I was asked to go to Matron's office — I went down a staff nurse and came back a sister. At that time, if a new sister was needed and the senior staff nurse was suitable, he or she automatically got the job.

At that time I didn't realise that I was destined to remain a sister. Many years later I was at home on a day off when I saw an advertisement in the paper which read: "Royal Victoria Hospital: Nursing Officer required for A & E, Intensive Care and Gynaecology". I requested a job description. One of the requirements was experience in intensive care, which I did not have, so I was not able to apply.

Liz McAllister, sister in charge of intensive care, applied for the job and got it. Helen Patterson, one of my sisters in A & E, met her one day at the hospital and remarked how lucky it was for Liz that she had experience in intensive care. Liz replied that it wasn't necessary for the job.

When Helen told me this, I suspected that an extra part had been added to my form to ensure that I didn't get the job. Liz had more experience than me, and would probably have got the position anyway, but I felt that I had been discriminated against on the grounds of my religion. I went straight to the Royal College of Nursing, where I met Paddy Sayer, Professional Officer. He wrote to the authorities at the Royal who replied saying that my forms came from the nursing department, but that others came from personnel, which explained the discrepancy.

The RCN would have supported me if I had wanted to pursue the claim, but after a lot of reflection I decided not to. I knew that a colleague who had successfully brought a discrimination complaint against the hospital had ended up being moved from a job she loved to one of the toughest positions in the hospital. I wanted to stay in A & E, where I believed that I was needed, doing the job I loved. So I stayed a sister.

One morning I was sitting in my office when I heard a dreadful racket. I went to investigate. A prisoner had been brought to the Royal under police escort to have an X-ray taken of his foot. He had given his escort the slip, run up the escalator to the Falls Road and vanished. We later heard a van had been waiting to make good his escape. The policemen were following in hot pursuit — well, hottish — running up the down escalator like something out of the Keystone Cops. It was the noise of their big boots ringing out on the metal steps that I had heard in my office.

In an A & E department it is important that the resuscitation room is near the entrance, so that the patient can be wheeled directly into it. Accordingly, our resuscitation room was at the door, first on the left, with three bays that could be screened off from each other. There were times when as many as seven patients occupied this area. The most modern medical appliances were housed in this room, and blood was stored there. As advances were made in medicine, we added more equipment, and acquired more knowledge. A very simple but important item amongst all this highly sophisticated apparatus was a large pair of scissors, which frequently had to be used to remove patients' clothing.

At the height of the Troubles the scissors often came into play. We once received word that an army Saracen had been attacked and an injured soldier was being brought to our department. Sister Helen Patterson and I prepared to receive a shot soldier, all equipment, including the scissors, at the ready. The patient was wheeled in, obviously in a great deal of pain, and we began cutting away his clothes. It was extremely difficult to cut off the soldier's bullet-proof vest, but we succeeded. Mr Rutherford tried to stop us in his own gentle way, but we didn't listen, and couldn't understand why he wasn't busy administering pain relief and putting up a drip. When the soldier was lying in his underpants, he managed to say that he had not been shot. The Saracen had gone over a ramp a bit too quickly and he had hit his back on one of the protrusions. He looked with dismay at the fragments of clothing lying on the floor. It was hard enough to get issued with a new pair of socks, he said, and he dreaded the quartermaster's reaction when he would see his uniform in ribbons. For a long time after, Helen and I were known among the ambulance men as the quickest strippers in the city.

Within the department, there was also a dressing room with three bays where outpatients who'd been treated in the department had their wounds dressed. (Nowadays this would be done by their GP.) To the left of the dressing room, there were five cubicles for treating ambulant patients with minor injuries such as cuts and bruises, minor fractures and burns. Behind these minor cubicles were review cubicles which were for patients who had been seen in casualty and discharged, but whom the doctors wanted to see again. One of these was a dental cubicle for use for out-of-hours emergencies when the dental hospital was closed.

We were very lucky to have the services of the Pink Ladies, so called because they wore pink overalls, who were the patients' guides in the hospital. These dedicated volunteers were usually middle-aged women from the community or retired staff. Based in outpatients, with one or two in the reception of our department, their duties were patient care, from directing patients and escorting them to appointments or X-rays to bringing cups of tea to relatives who had been waiting for a long time. Jean Shaw, in charge of the Pink Ladies, was a valuable member of the A & E team. When she was on duty, I knew everyone was being looked after. I asked for her help on many occasions when I was going to the mortuary with relatives to identify a body. She sat with bereaved relatives, sometimes all day, or if a patient was in theatre, she liaised with staff and family. She did not leave the relatives until she could do no more for them. A tower of strength, she treated everyone with equal care, and anything told to her was in strict confidence.

Our observation ward, at the back of Level 2, was for any patient whose symptoms were not severe enough for admission to the main wards, but who required 24-hour observation. These patients would be suffering, for example, from chest pains or concussion, or would be recovering from an overdose. If they weren't fit for discharge within twenty-four hours, they were admitted to the main wards. Far away from all the action, the observation ward was especially useful for patients in emotional shock, who had been caught up in riots or explosions, or any other kind of disaster. They would be kept here with some experienced staff on hand to ensure that they did not also have some underlying injury. There were two three-bedded wards, two single wards, two bathrooms and a kitchen. Two casualty theatres were attached to this ward. It was well designed for the purpose and a big improvement on the Nissen hut that had been our old observation ward.

Beyond the observation ward was the fracture clinic, which had cubicles, treatment rooms, plaster rooms, theatres and offices. A very busy department, it received patients from our department as well as from other hospitals.

We were very fortunate we had moved into our new department before the onslaught of the Troubles. As a team, we had four months to become fully used to all aspects of the new unit. It was as if someone had known that the Troubles were going to start.

Planning for disaster

What is a disaster? Mr Rutherford defined it not by the number of casualties involved, but as an incident that required extraordinary mobilisation in a department.

Each emergency service and hospital must have a Disaster Plan. The plan for the Royal was updated in 1969 when we moved to the new unit. At the time we thought we would never need it, but we were soon to realise how vital it was. We never had a rehearsal, but through the years we had to cope with the real thing often enough.

The plan provided each department with a relevant wall chart showing all the key points with which every member of staff was expected to be familiar, so that they would know exactly what to do in an emergency and where to find the emergency equipment. The preamble stated:

The plan is intended to be a fluid procedure, which should enable the right number and category of staff to be mobilized according to the needs of each disaster. Flexibility of response is achieved by having a Control Team which monitors the situation as it develops, and mobilizes suitable hospital staff.

The control team consisted of the group medical administrator, assistant group medical administrator, assistant director of nursing, casualty consultant and casualty sister. We all carried pagers, even when we went off duty. When we were unavailable, on holiday for instance, we passed them on to a deputy.

Each disaster is different, depending on the time of day, the day of the week, the number of casualties, the number critically injured, seriously injured, or walking wounded, the number of staff on duty and the number of seriously ill patients already in the department. Casualties often arrived at the door in private vehicles, including taxis; in army vehicles and army ambulances; and, once, casualties arrived in a Belfast Corporation bus. In many such cases, patients came in without any prior warning, and we were kept so busy treating them that we had no time to inform anyone of their arrival.

When we got word of a major incident in advance, we had to inform the switchboard staff. They implemented the Disaster Plan and set off the bleeps. We also informed our own doctors and nurses, and nursing administration, and cleared the department of all non-emergency patients. Minor patients were told about the situation, and were advised that they might have to go home and come back later. We prepared our resuscitation room, checking blood supplies, running through intravenous infusions, leaving out the large scissors for the cutting of clothes. We informed our nurse in the observation ward, which would be used for distressed patients. In those days there were specific days for surgical and medical take-in. The surgical take-in ward cleared beds in preparation for emergency admissions. Patients could be transferred to other wards, other hospitals, or sent home. Taxis could be used to transport them if necessary. It was the responsibility of security staff to keep all corridors, roadways and entrances to the department clear, and to keep out television reporters and the press. The large gym on Level 3 could be made into a ward, with camp beds and blankets to be used for patients waiting for discharge or going to other hospitals.

A hospital administrator liaised with relatives and the emergency room. In a disaster situation, the receptionists came round and made out regular documentation for each patient in triplicate — one copy to stay with the patient, one for the files, and one for the administrator to enable him or her to give out information to relatives and police. Our aim was to have a brief indication of the condition of the patient and his or her disposal available as rapidly as possible.

Although it didn't form part of the plan, an important part of our strategy for coping with disasters was to keep everything the same as it was on an ordinary day — no different uniforms, procedures or documentation. There was less likelihood of mistakes if staff followed their usual routines.

When it was put into action, the Disaster Plan imposed order on what would otherwise have been chaotic situations. Our plan was seen to be very successful, and was requested by, despatched to and adopted by many other hospitals across the UK.

The Malvern Street murder

If the start of the Troubles in 1969 took us by surprise, then the Malvern Street shootings in June 1966 came like a bolt from the blue. Our patients on Saturday nights were mostly inebriated, or suffering injuries from domestic fights and road traffic accidents. There were also the usual medical and surgical emergencies. Shootings in Belfast just never happened.

I was in charge in casualty that Saturday night. It had been quiet and in the early hours of Sunday morning we were sitting, relaxed and chatting. The telephone rang. It was ambulance control to say there had been a shooting in Malvern Street, and two ambulances had been sent out. I was astounded to hear this news, and when I informed the surgical registrar, Alan Gurd, he also was very taken aback. He told me to keep him informed.

Ambulance control phoned again to say that one young man was dead, but they were bringing in two wounded youths. Neither was critically injured, although both required immediate surgery. Dr Gurd called in Mr Ernest Morrison, his consultant, and they were busy in theatre for many hours. Both young men survived, although one had been struck by six bullets.

51

Peter Ward, aged eighteen, had died from a wound to the heart. His body was put in an ambulance and brought to the hospital. A doctor went out to certify him dead and he was anointed before he was moved to the mortuary. The place was swarming with police inside and out. His mother arrived at the hospital accompanied by her younger son and Canon Patrick Murphy from St Peter's parish. In our observation ward we told Mrs Ward that her son had been shot dead. His distraught brother, only sixteen years old, ran down the corridor, through the yard in front of casualty and out the gate on to the Grosvenor Road. He was going to Malvern Street, he said, to avenge his brother's death. We brought him back to his mother.

Peter Ward and his friends were barmen in a hotel in the city. When they finished work, they had gone for a drink in the Malvern Arms off the Protestant Shankill Road. They were identified as Catholics by a group of men in the Ulster Volunteer Force, who opened fire on them when they left the bar.

This was the first time I ever had any experience of an event like this. How do you treat gunshot wounds? We found over the years that initial resuscitation is the same for gunshot victims as that given to any patient with multiple injuries, for instance someone injured in a road traffic accident. The patient must be completely undressed, as something can be missed if they are clothed. That is why large scissors were such an important part of our equipment in the resuscitation room. One of the first things we had to do was administer intravenous fluids, and often blood too. We also had to control bleeding from wounds. If there was damage to a patient's neck, we moved them very carefully from the ambulance trolley to the hospital trolley, with one person holding the head and neck and approximately four others the body, lifting on command. If a patient was unconscious or having difficulty breathing, we would intubate them to maintain a clear airway and administer oxygen.

One of the most important things to do was to reassure the patient; we were all conscious that it was very frightening for patients to lie in a resuscitation room with so many people and so much activity around them. In some cases, if enough staff were available, one nurse would remain with the patient until they left the department, especially if the patient had been blinded or had injuries to the eye. We administered pain relief as soon as it was safe. Sometimes we could do this immediately, but if seriously ill patients are given pain relief too soon, they may not be able to tell the doctor what happened or where they are injured. History is very important, whether from the patient, the paramedic or a bystander. Continuous monitoring of vital functions is essential, using the Glasgow Coma Scale to ascertain the level of consciousness. While the treatment in casualty may be the same for gunshot victims as it is for those injured in traffic accidents, the subsequent treatment in theatre and intensive care will be different for each patient, depending on the injuries and, for victims of shootings, on the calibre of the weapon.

The Malvern Street murder, as it came to be known, was not the first shooting of the Troubles, however. That had happened a month earlier, on 27 May, when John Scullion, a 28-year-old Catholic storeman, was attacked by a UVF gang in west Belfast. He was singing on his way back from a club. After he was attacked, he managed to make his way home and get into the house, but he collapsed at the top of the stairs. The authorities claimed he had been stabbed, although local people insisted he had been shot. After suffering several heart attacks he died on 11 June and was buried in Milltown cemetery. The controversy surrounding the cause of his death was not settled until his body was exhumed almost two weeks later, when an autopsy revealed that he had indeed been shot.

And prior to the Scullion attack, on 7 May the home of Matilda Gould, an elderly Protestant widow, was set on fire by members of the UVF during an attempt to petrol bomb the Catholic-owned bar next door. She was badly burned, dying from her injuries seven weeks later, on 27 June, the day after Peter Ward was killed. She may have been the third person to die in the Troubles, but she was the first to be injured. The UVF was responsible for all three deaths that year.

In the days and nights that followed the Malvern Street incident, we continued to treat medical and surgical emergencies and all trauma patients as usual. But the psychological effect of this killing on staff was profound. You cannot compare the deliberate attempt to kill a fellow human being to a death caused by accident. I wondered about the men who had committed this attack, so I went to court to listen to the trial, where three men were given life sentences for the killing. Gusty Spence, later to become a prominent figure in the UVF, was among those convicted. The thing that always struck me about the many murderers I have seen through the years is that you would pass them on the street and never notice them; they are mostly insignificant-looking characters.

Undoubtedly, the worst part of emergency nursing is having to tell relatives that their loved ones have died. How much worse when you have to tell a mother that her eighteen-year-old son has been murdered? I did not know then that I would be called upon to repeat this distressing task many times over the next twenty-two years, telling husbands, wives, mothers, fathers, sons, daughters and friends of the tragic death of a loved one. We talked about the Malvern Street murder for many days to come, little thinking it would be the first of many such incidents.

The beginning of the Troubles and internment

Since 1967 the Northern Ireland Civil Rights Association had been campaigning for an end to discrimination against the Catholic community. Its march in Derry in October 1968 received worldwide media attention when the Royal Ulster Constabulary (RUC) batoned the marchers, injuring many. At the start of 1969, People's Democracy civil rights activists organised a march from Belfast to Derry, which, despite a police escort, was ambushed by loyalists at Burntollet Bridge. Again many marchers were injured and riots ensued in Derry. As the year progressed, tension mounted and when violence erupted once more in Derry during the Apprentice Boys parade in August, escalating to the so-called Battle of the Bogside, rioting spread to Belfast and other towns. Catholic houses were burned, leaving many homeless, and as the violence spiralled out of control, British troops were deployed on the streets of Derry and Belfast.

By the end of 1969, 18 people had died, 14 of them civilians, and hundreds had been injured. The following year 28 died, including 19 civilians. But none of these years was comparable to the carnage of 1971; the death toll that year was 180, including 94 civilians, the vast majority of deaths and serious injuries occurring after the introduction in August of internment without trial.

Internment means different things to different people: to some it was just a few hours of mayhem on an August morning in 1971; to others it meant weeks and months of anxiety, pain, uncertainty and worry about the safety of relatives. Some of the men who were interned subsequently suffered years of physical and mental illness.

Sanctioned by British Prime Minister Ted Heath, at the instigation of the Unionist government led by Brian Faulkner, the measure was introduced against the advice of the army, who thought, rightly as it turned out, that the situation would only get worse as a result.

On 9 August, in the early hours of the morning, the army swooped on the Catholic areas across the North. My brother Brian and his wife Moira were on holiday, staying with me in Newington Avenue. We were wakened by the sound of shouting, screaming, gunfire and the screeching of army Saracens. There was a terrible commotion on the New Lodge Road and in Ardoyne. In the quiet darkness of the night we could hear the noise coming from all over the city.

That night almost three hundred and fifty men were taken from their homes to internment camps, many of whom had no connection with the IRA. One Englishman who had been in the merchant navy all his life and who lived near me was lifted and interned until the authorities discovered their mistake a few days later. Over one hundred men were released after two days; the rest were interned on a prison ship on Belfast Lough, in Crumlin Road jail or at Long Kesh. Only Catholics were lifted; no attempt was made to intern members of the loyalist UVF, although that organisation had been responsible for killings and bombings. Many of the internees were ill-treated. The European Court of Human Rights later ruled that some internees had been subjected to "inhumane and degrading treatment".

Internment provoked widespread violence, especially in the city, where fierce fighting broke out and burning barricades were erected. Brian and Moira could not get away fast enough and did not return to Belfast for many years. I drove them to the airport. On the way, we passed a Catholic pub on fire, being looted by a crowd. The police stood by watching.

On leaving the airport, I went to a church hall in Glengormley that had been set up as a refugee centre. Women and children were there, worried about their menfolk. Some people required medication — insulin for the diabetics, inhalers, oxygen and various prescribed medicines. Since Faulkner's election in March as leader of the Unionist Party, internment had been expected, so these refugee centres were well organised with supplies, blankets, food and children's necessities. There were many volunteers. The Irish government also set up refugee centres, mostly in army camps near the border. People flocked over the border, by car, bus, train, and on foot. Their homes had been attacked and whole streets were burned. A total of seven thousand people fled their homes and crossed the border to safety.

Once I'd done everything that I could at the church hall, I went to the Royal. The A & E department was crowded with wounded and dying patients. The first dead body we received was of a woman who had been shot in Ballymurphy, a Catholic area near the hospital. Twenty-three people were shot dead in the space of a few days. In Ballymurphy, Father Gerry Weston, the Catholic padre from the Parachute Regiment, anointed some of the dead and dying. At that time we had the Parachute Regiment's doctor working in the depart-ment. I said: "You have a great system. Your soldiers shoot them, your padre anoints them and you look after them in hospital." The priest was among seven killed at the regiment's headquarters at Aldershot in an Official IRA car-bomb attack the following year.

At eight the next morning an ambulance arrived at the door with two more dead bodies. One was Father Hugh Mullan, who was a friend of my brother's, and the other was a young man who had gone to help him. Father Mullan was dressed in his black soutane and looked very peaceful. He had gone to anoint a casualty in a field at Ballymurphy and had been shot by the army.

We received a patient from one of the internment camps. His body was badly bruised, black and blue all over. The doctor examined him and took photographs of his injuries. He asked me to witness the examination, and I signed the document and the photographs. This was one of the cases later raised at the European Court of Human Rights.

During this time, men continued to be rounded up and interned — prior to Direct Rule in March 1972, the number of internees stood at 924 — and there were shootings and rioting every day. Homes were destroyed and people were terrified. It was difficult for them to get into the hospital; it was even difficult for the ambulances. We were kept busy round the clock. All holidays were cancelled. Eventually, I was so exhausted my eyes were bloodshot, for the first and last time in my life. Matron took one look at me and told me to take some leave to recuperate. Aileen Greene, the sister in charge of the orthopaedic ward, and I went to Edinburgh, but it took a couple of days for us to unwind and to start enjoying our break.

The army had been right. The Troubles intensified after internment, and we were kept busy night and day.

McGurk's bar

It happened in the season of good cheer, of peace and goodwill towards all men. On the night of 4 December 1971 a bomb exploded in McGurk's bar, in North Queen Street. There was no warning. A Catholic-owned pub in a Catholic area, just a few hundred yards from a staunchly Protestant area, the bar was run by Paddy McGurk, a quiet, gentle countryman, and his family; they had living quarters upstairs. Fifteen people were killed, including Paddy McGurk's wife, Philomena, and his daughter, Maria, aged fourteen. Two other women and a thirteen-year-old schoolboy died in the blast, as well ten men, including a pensioner. Thirteen people were injured, some seriously.

I was driving home from the hospital up Clifton Street when I heard the explosion. I had been given special permission to travel in uniform for safety, because of the dangerous situation in the city. I did not know where the blast had happened, but I knew it was close. I went on home, about five minutes away. The neighbours were on the street and when I learned that a bomb had exploded in a bar in North Queen Street, I went to see if I could help. Still in uniform, I parked in

Donegall Street, as North Queen Street had been cordoned off by the emergency services. I was allowed through. It was cold and dark and there was an eerie silence. Some distance along the street, I saw flashing blue lights. I approached, expecting to see the shell of a building, but there were only bricks and rubble.

Many people were on top of the wreckage, digging desperately with their bare hands. No order, just desperation. The scene was lit only by the lights from the ambulances and the street lighting. Beyond the devastation I could make out the outline of people watching and praying. Pat Fleming, the casualty sister from the Mater Hospital, and Sheila Doran from the Children's Hospital, together with the local doctors and priests, had been among the first to arrive on the scene. Bricks were lifted and reached back from hand to hand in a human chain. The ruins were smouldering, and there were bursts of flames from gas leaks, forcing the rescuers to abandon their efforts and jump back to safety. Some bodies had already been recovered and some casualties had gone to hospital. Two people were trapped in a snug. I hoped they had been overcome by fumes and not burned to death.

It was hard to believe that until a very short time ago this had been a public house, with customers enjoying a quiet drink, and, upstairs, a home where a mother and her children were spending a usual Saturday night. Philomena McGurk had her apron on when her body was brought into the Royal. She might have been preparing the Sunday dinner. Roddy McCorley, a 27-year-old merchant navy man, had been drinking in

62

the bar. He had his leg blown off. Pat Fleming took him to the hospital in an ambulance, applying pressure to his leg, whispering an act of contrition in his ear and keeping him alive until they arrived at the Royal.

Mr Rutherford arrived on the scene. He had treated the first casualties at the hospital, and because of the delay in rescuing any more, he had come out to help. There were instructions and counter-instructions and he tried to organise rescue efforts. There was a feeling of helplessness but also an overriding feeling of anger. I was not sure what to do — it is one thing to treat patients in a well-lit, well-equipped casualty department and quite another to treat them on the street with nothing to hand. The Parachute Regiment arrived with lifting equipment and more lighting. A cry went up. A boy had been found alive. I shouted at everyone to be careful. I could not envisage anyone coming out of that rubble without very serious injuries. He escaped with a leg wound requiring five stitches; but these survivors, of course, live on with invisible scars.

As the rescue continued through the night a crowd gathered at the corner of Brougham Street and North Queen Street, a flash point between the Protestant and Catholic areas. Cars were wrecked, missiles thrown and windows broken. Then a gun battle started. An army major was shot and died a few days later as a result of his injuries. An ambulance had been dispatched to collect some casualties; the ambulance men asked me to go with them. We parked beside an entry in Brougham Street and they left to bring in the casualties, shouting back to me to turn off the lights. I crawled into the front of the ambulance and pulled a few switches. Clearly not the right ones, as the ambulance men later said that when they looked back at the ambulance, it was like seeing the Blackpool illuminations in the middle of a gun battle.

The first casualty was a soldier; he had been injured by his own Saracen. His only worry was the hospital he was going to. I do not know what he had been told. Maybe he just did not want to go into the military wing at Musgrave Park Hospital. The soldiers we got in as patients hated being transferred there, not because of the medical attention but because patients were still expected to observe strict army discipline — standing to attention and making their own beds if they were able. They preferred to stay at the Royal, with our nurses looking after them.

The next casualty was a policeman who had been shot, but he was not seriously hurt. The third and last was a drunk man who had lost his carry-out of drink up the entry, and he was not prepared to leave it behind and go to any so-and-so hospital. He was oblivious to the fact that he had nearly been killed. A bullet had grazed his head and he was bleeding profusely. It was a wonder that he could see anything the way the blood was running down his face. The nurses in A & E used to tell me how strict I was, and say: "Put on your Sister's face and go out and chase those drunks." I tried my stony face on this man, who did not seem to be very intimidated by it, but at least he got into the ambulance. With bullets still flying, I urged the ambulance men to make a fast exit, and we left taking the three casualties with us.

It was the early hours of the morning when we reached the Royal. Staff Nurse Helen Lowry took one look at me and said that *I* needed resuscitation — and she gave me some hot, sweet tea. Black from the smoke and debris, I washed and changed before going back on duty. By then, the drunk patient had disappeared. He had made a run for it as soon as he had been cleaned up, risking life and limb to get back to his carry-out. The department was busy that night, for as well as the casualties from the explosion we had the usual number of Saturday night patients.

Paddy McGurk was one of our patients and he kept asking for his family. He thought at first that they had not been in the house, saying, "Thank God they are not back from St Patrick's Church", where they had gone to confession. As time went on and they did not appear, he began to fear the worst. Finally a relative went down to the mortuary with Mr Rutherford and identified the bodies of Mrs McGurk, her brother John Colton, and her young daughter, Marie. How do you tell a man that he has lost his wife, his daughter and his brother-in-law?

John Irvine had been in the pub that evening with his wife, Kathleen, and two friends, sitting at a corner table. He was the only survivor of the four of them. Buried under debris, he held his wife's hand until it slipped from his grasp. Her body lay in the mortuary; I think he knew she was dead. If a loved one is ill and the family is expecting the death, it is bad enough. For it to

65

be the result of an explosion of a bomb deliberately placed by another human being to cause carnage, it must be very difficult to bear. Paddy McGurk and John Irvine were admitted to our observation ward. Paddy's sons survived with minor injuries: John, just ten years old, was pulled from the rubble with an injury to his finger, and Gerard was admitted to the orthopaedic ward with a broken leg; he was later moved to the observation ward to be with his father. John Irvine was a lovely man and attended our dressing room after his discharge. He had eleven stitches and bruising all over his back. He was most appreciative of anything we did for him.

Around three in the morning an ambulance arrived with two charred bodies — the remains of the people trapped in the snug. A young doctor went out to certify them dead before they were taken to the mortuary. He told us later that he could not get the smell of burnt flesh out of his clothes or off his skin for days, and the incident stayed with him for many months. I went home for a few hours and as I drove up our avenue I was stopped by an army patrol. The soldiers belonged to the regiment whose major had been shot that night.

When I went back on duty, a great many visitors were waiting to see Paddy McGurk — there were family members, of course, but there were also politicians and Church figures. In the end, we had to stop all visitors except family. Frequently you see television reports and photographs in newspapers of some important person visiting the survivors of a disaster. Some may be genuinely concerned, but I am convinced that others make an appearance to drum up a bit of publicity for themselves. The patients are usually too distressed and exhausted to talk to them. We protected the family from the media during their stay in hospital as best we could. But it was clear that the television cameras and press photographers would be waiting for them the moment they were ready to leave the hospital.

The following day, when an IRA explosion and subsequent fire on the Dublin Road caused the gable wall of the Salvation Army headquarters to collapse, Mamie Thompson was killed, and other members of the Salvation Army, including her husband, Samuel, were injured. He was admitted to our observation ward. There were now three bereaved widowers in one ward. The nurse in charge, a lovely, gentle girl, said to me, "Sister, I don't know how I'm going to get through this day." I said, "I don't know whether I can either." The doctor said, "Why don't you take 5 mg of Valium?" We got a tablet out and looked at it, and in the end we broke it in two and took half each. We were worried that we would either fall asleep or be drowsy all day. It had no effect. We survived the day and were thankful. No tablet ever again.

Less than a week later, on 11 December, a bomb in a Shankill Road furniture shop killed two men and two small children — a little girl just two years old and a baby boy of seventeen months who were in their prams outside the shop when the bomb exploded. Nineteen people were injured, some seriously. It was reported that the bomb had been planted by the IRA in retaliation for the bombing of McGurk's bar. The ambulance men brought the two men and the babies into our department. Because we have the Children's Hospital in the grounds, we do not treat children under twelve years old and therefore do not have small trolleys. The dead men were put on ordinary trolleys and a baby was placed on each, lying inside the curve of each man's arm, close together. One of our consultants went down to the morgue with the father of one of the children. He stood crying as the man identified his child; he said he was thinking of his own children.

How did we feel when the department was cleared and all the patients had been treated and all the dead had been identified? The simple answer to that question is, we were devastated. There had been no time to sit down and mourn. We had learned to rely on one another, and there was great teamwork, but we were drained, mentally and physically. I had never been at the scene of an explosion before and I had never experienced anything as bad as that night at the ruins of McGurk's bar and its aftermath at the hospital. But as a nurse, no matter how you feel, you must appear calm. And when you are in charge, you cannot let yourself panic or everyone else will panic also. But the horrific sights and the distress of patients and relatives take their toll. I did not sleep for a couple of nights. Some incidents affect you more than others, and the carnage at McGurk's bar will always stand out in my memory.

It was first reported by police that the IRA had caused the explosion at the bar, leaving a bomb in transit. And a few years later, in his book *Bombs Have No Pity*, Lieutenant-Colonel George Styles was still claiming that the explosion at McGurk's was "another own goal" by the IRA. With reports like these from official sources, it took some time for the truth to emerge. It was not until 1978 that a member of the UVF was tried for the bombing and convicted; he received fifteen life sentences.

Christmas decorations were hanging in our department and on Mr Rutherford's office door we had placed a sign: "Peace on earth and goodwill to all men". This office was used to inform relatives of the deaths of their loved ones, so we took the greeting down. There was very little peace and goodwill to be had in Belfast.

1972: The Abercorn, Donegall Street and Bloody Friday

The situation worsened considerably in 1972, which had the highest death toll (496) of all the years of the Troubles. The year started badly. January ended with Bloody Sunday, when thirteen unarmed civil rights marchers in Derry were shot dead by the Parachute Regiment, and a fourteenth was fatally wounded. IRA recruitment accelerated as a result. Loyalist killings of Catholics intensified. IRA car-bombs — a new tactic — caused death, injury and widespread panic in Belfast and in towns across the North. Two bomb attacks in March were particularly horrific.

On the first Saturday of the month, a bright, sunny afternoon, the centre of Belfast was packed with people shopping. They may have been uneasy; the city was a dangerous place to be, and there had been shootings, bomb scares and two explosions that day. The A & E department at the Royal was experiencing an unexpected and unusual lull. There were no patients. Five nurses — three of whom were students — and the staff nurse in charge, Norma Grindle, were enjoying the break. There were also two junior doctors on duty — as it was a weekend, there was a minimum of doctors on duty and no surplus nurses, just the number required on duty in each unit. And on the levels above the department, the outpatient clinics were closed. I was on holiday that day and the other casualty sister was off duty for the afternoon.

There were three patients waiting for transport in the observation ward. When Norma rang ambulance control to find out why the patients were still waiting, ambulance control told her that they had no time to talk to her — there had been a big explosion downtown which had caused many, many casualties, and they were all on their way to the Royal. Norma hurried back down to the office and telephoned Matron's office to ask for help. As she was on the phone, being told that there were no nurses to spare, she heard the sirens of the first ambulances arriving at the department.

The Abercorn, a popular city-centre restaurant, was situated between two narrow streets off Cornmarket. It was crowded that afternoon, with customers waiting for tables, and 250 people were in a cabaret club upstairs. Without thought for man, woman or child, a 51b bomb was planted under a table at the back.

Anne Owens and her friend Janet Bereen were having a coffee when the bomb exploded without warning. They were killed outright. Over one hundred people were hurt in the blast, some with horrendous injuries. Two sisters, Rosaleen and Jennifer McNern, both lost their legs, and Rosaleen lost part of her right arm as well. She was to be married shortly. Jimmy Stewart was also about to be married. He had called into the Abercorn before meeting up with his fiancée; he lost both legs. Irene Arnold was working her last day as a waitress; she lost both legs and an eye. Many people were injured by parts of flying crockery and cutlery, some even had bits of furniture embedded in their bodies. There were injuries from broken glass both inside and outside the restaurant. Because of the crowds of people in the narrow streets outside, evacuating the casualties was difficult.

In the club above the restaurant the floor shook and the lights went out when the bomb went off. A few people were slightly injured in the initial panic but the MC continued speaking to them to calm things down and the band played. All 250 were evacuated safely down the fire escape.

The injuries of the patients arriving at A & E were horrific: limbs blown off, eye injuries, multiple trauma. Patients were lying everywhere, in all the cubicles and in the corridors. A senior nurse came down from administration, followed shortly afterwards by the assistant matron, Miss Florence Betty. When Miss Betty saw the seriousness of the situation, she got the sister or nurse in charge from each department to come and help at once. Miss Betty told Norma, "You are in charge. I do not know this department; just tell me what to do." It was unusual, to say the least, for sisters to take instructions from a staff nurse, which didn't make things any easier for Norma. Most of these nurses had not worked in the department before and they certainly got a baptism of fire. The Abercorn explosion was not immediately declared a disaster, so our Disaster Plan was not put into operation. Mr Rutherford later had a meeting with ambulance control to ensure this didn't happen again. If the plan had been activated, it would have considerably helped the nurse in charge. When I returned from holiday, the matron told me how well Norma had coped; it was the sign of a good department, she said, when the staff managed so well when the sister in charge was absent.

One of our consultant anaesthetists, Dr Minty Bereen, was working in theatre, tending to the victims, unaware that his daughter had been killed. A radiographer, she had been working in the Royal that morning, and had gone into town in the afternoon. Her father only learned about her death when he came off duty.

The photographs taken of the injuries that day are among the worst I have ever seen. Many were taken in the department and in theatre and show amputated limbs lying on towels. One photograph shows a woman with the leg of a table through her own leg. Standing with her is the sister from the medical ward, who looks to be in a state of complete shock. The staff must have had nightmares for months.

This was a truly evil act — two young women killed and others whose bodies were badly mutilated. How these unfortunate people coped with the rest of their lives we can only begin to imagine. One young man who was caught up in the explosion summed it up:

The public tend to say three dead, thirteen injured, how terrible, but they really think about the dead and forget about thirteen injured who might want to die when they find out the extent of their injuries. How many will be scarred for life and carry around invisible scars which none of us will see?

It brought to mind what another young victim had said in the aftermath of McGurk's bar: "We are news one day and history the next."

Before the month was out, on 20 March, just sixteen days after the attack on the Abercorn, a massive 200 lb car-bomb exploded in Donegall Street, and within the space of an hour 150 people were brought to our department — the largest number of casualties we ever received in so short a space of time. Police had received conflicting warnings about where the device was placed and many who were caught in the blast were being shepherded from one street, where they would have been safer, into the path of the bomb. Six people were killed at the scene and one man, whose leg had been blown off, died in the resuscitation room.

Our Disaster Plan went into action. A senior casualty nurse or the casualty consultant saw each patient as they arrived by ambulance. Thirty were seriously injured either by the explosion itself or by shrapnel and flying glass. Seven patients in the resuscitation room were looked after by teams of experienced doctors and nurses. The man who died there was transferred to our teaching room, now at the back of the unit. All the

74

seriously injured were kept in our department and resuscitated before going to theatre, the intensive care unit, the fracture clinic or the wards. Fifty patients were admitted. Sixty patients required suturing and were later discharged. The remaining patients were emotionally shocked and went home in due course.

With such an influx, the department was crowded with patients; they were everywhere — all the cubicles were occupied, as well as the dressing room, and the observation ward; the fracture clinic cubicles were also used, until injured patients with fractures were ready to go to them. As nurse in charge I never got involved with any one patient. I followed procedure, constantly making rounds of all the casualties, keeping an overall picture of the whole department, making sure patients were being adequately cared for with the correct number and grades of staff, and ensuring no unwanted personnel were in the department. At a time like this, other hospital staff rushed down to the department, some out of curiosity, others out of concern in case they knew someone who had been brought in, and this was sometimes more of a hindrance than a help. We did accept aid from other departments and other staff, of course, and that day doctors and senior medical students sutured, the venereologist came down from the level above us to lend a hand, and the dermatologist resuscitated in the dressing room, putting up an infusion for a patient whose leg was almost severed.

Relatives were kept in the waiting room and a liaison officer gave out all necessary information as soon as it was possible to do so. The receptionists made out forms in triplicate with all relevant details. If a name was unknown, they used the letters A to Z to temporarily identify patients until their names were ascertained.

The surgeon in charge made the difficult decision on theatre priority. We followed the rule that those critically injured with hope of survival were given first priority. Those less seriously injured were resuscitated, transferred to a ward and sent to theatre later. Patients whose injuries were not compatible with life would wait.

Mr Rutherford did not approve of this rule, and indeed our prognosis was not always correct. God sometimes had other ideas. In 1975, during an IRA feud, we had eight patients in the department who had been shot. They all needed to go to surgery and there were several theatres working. One man had been shot a great many times and after we had resuscitated him with intravenous infusions and drains to his chest, he was brought up to the anaesthetic room of theatre but not rushed into an operation as it was thought he would not survive. But he did survive and eventually went into theatre, and was transferred to the intensive care unit. He was sitting up in bed two days later and made a full recovery.

After our patients, our main concern was the relatives, getting information to them quickly, talking to them if their loved ones were critically ill or had died. We tried to let them see their relatives before they were rushed to theatre — it might be for the last time. I was always very sorry when this was not possible.

With the political situation rapidly deteriorating, the Unionist government at Stormont was prorogued and Direct Rule introduced on 28 March. In July an IRA ceasefire broke down after two weeks, and just over a fortnight later, on 21 July, the organisation detonated twenty bombs across the city in approximately the space of one hour. Eleven people were killed and 130 were injured, some horribly mutilated.

There had been occasions when all we received at the department were body parts in black plastic bags, but nothing could have prepared us for Bloody Friday. With the town in chaos and so many roads closed, the ambulances had difficulty getting to the hospitals. I was in a hairdresser's on the Grosvenor Road, opposite the entrance gate to the Royal, with the sister from intensive care and the sister from the vascular unit. We saw and heard the ambulances leaving the Royal and started back to the hospital immediately, with our hair still wet and in rollers. We arrived with the first casualties.

I remember almost all my experiences of coping with explosions and horrific injuries, but I have very little memory of Bloody Friday even though I was on duty throughout it all, from the admission of the first casualty until every patient had been looked after. I remember a clergyman looking for his son who had been near the scene of one of the worst blasts, at shops on the Cavehill Road. The matron took him down to the mortuary and he identified his son only by his Scout buckle. In another blast, one of our sisters was blown off her feet going home. I found two of my friends lying on trolleys; thankfully they only had minor injuries. They had been in different parts of town. These things I remember.

In my career I had had to cope with other traumatic incidents. I had been handed body parts; once I was given only skin attached to an army badge from an explosive expert who was killed dismantling a bomb; there were the two dead babies brought in to the department from the explosion on the Shankill Road. Once, I went to an ambulance with the doctor to certify a patient dead, and all that was there was a head — the sole remains of a victim after an explosion in a house. Another day a milkman carried in a little boy who had found a gun under a car and pulled the trigger. I was holding him; he was kicking and screaming, and the doctor could not see any obvious injury. I looked down at my apron and saw bits of brain. We took him into our resuscitation room and quickly got an anaesthetist. He was one of the lucky ones. He had some weakness in his left leg and arm for a while but gradually he made a good recovery. I remember all these and many more equally traumatic events: I cannot account for my hazy recollection of Bloody Friday.

Television reports later showed scenes of devastation and members of the emergency services collecting body parts and putting them into black plastic bags. Three people had been killed in the Cavehill Road explosion, including two women, one a mother of seven, and the young fourteen-year-old son of the Reverend Joseph Parker. And six people had died when a car-bomb exploded in the busy bus station in Oxford Street, which also caused many of the worst injuries. As people watched these evening reports with a growing sense of horror and revulsion, many thought that perhaps the bombers would stop at this, but they did not.

Long Kesh

Long Kesh internment camp, later called the Maze prison, is situated near Lisburn, about half an hour's drive from Belfast. I was at home one October day in 1974 when I received word from the hospital that there had been riots at the camp. I was told there had been much destruction and many casualties were at the Royal. I quickly drove over to the hospital. The place was surrounded by police and army personnel, who were stopping everyone and refusing entry. I was greeted by a soldier who attempted to stop me from entering my own department. I told him who I was and walked on past him.

The ambulance room was swarming with police, even though it turned out there were only two patients in the department at that time. One had an escort of two prison officers. The other was a very frightened "ordinary" patient who had no idea what was going on. Outside in the reception area about two hundred women were in a very anxious mood, excitable and abusive. Rumours were flying about that men in the camp had been seriously injured and even killed. Looking for their menfolk, they swarmed, shouting, into the resuscitation room. One English consultant who tried to quell the disturbance was given his pedigree back to early days, the women calling him a "bloody Brit". Someone called me a "red bitch of a Prod" because of my red uniform. I have been called many names in my day but I consider this to be the best.

An army sergeant, the most senior member of the security forces present, ordered our senior consultants not to give out any information. I asked the police to leave the ambulance room as they were only making the situation worse, and they withdrew. One young soldier was running through the department and the reception area pointing his gun at everyone, calling the women the foulest names. I told him to leave as he was only causing trouble and was in danger of shooting someone. I escorted him down to the observation ward and told him to stay there. When I got back, I asked the crowd to make way for a patient coming out of theatre after an orthopaedic operation. I explained that he was recovering from an anaesthetic, and we had to get him back to his ward. One woman shouted: "Don't kid us, Nurse. He's suffering from CS gas." I went into theatre and asked the anaesthetist what on earth he was using.

I became very worried for the safety of the staff — one nurse had been hit over the head with an umbrella. I decided that we should leave the department. I locked the one patient we had left in a cubicle with two nurses; the rest of us retreated to the sisters' changing room. I opened a bottle of brandy, which we had been given as a present, and poured some into paper cups for everyone — student nurses, sisters and doctors alike. Apparently it was the best cognac; one doctor said he could face anything after that. Just as well then, as he was hit over the head the moment he appeared outside the door.

Eventually, the hospital authorities decided to give out all available information, against the orders of the security forces. The hospital had only received two patients from the riots. When the consultants spoke to the women, things calmed down. At a hospital meeting after this incident it was decided always to adhere to our policy of giving out information as quickly as possible to relatives. It was also agreed that if such an incident occurred again, we would request that a more senior member of the security forces be put in charge.

It was not until I read *The Flames of Long Kesh 15–16 October 1974*, by Father Denis Faul and Father Raymond Murray that I realised the enormity of it all. Many people were injured, but received only the most basic medical treatment from unqualified staff. Many of those who were more seriously injured never saw a hospital. Some were taken to hospitals outside the city. I also heard rumours that some of those who were seriously injured were taken straight to the wards, and that no admission forms or documentation were ever made out for them.

Casualities from the civil disturbances

Over a three-year period, on forty-eight occasions, the Royal received patients with multiple injuries from explosions. There were fifteen occasions when riots caused disaster situations. Between October 1970 and November 1974, a total of 2,040 patients were admitted to the hospital as a result of civil disturbance.

Situated as it was in what might be termed a battle zone, and in close proximity to the city centre, casualties would arrive at the hospital very soon after being injured. Our modern, well-equipped department was backed up by an intensive care unit, and orthopaedic, burns, general surgery, ophthalmology, maxillofacial surgery, thoracic, neurosurgical, and ENT departments, which meant that there was the shortest of intervals between arrival at the hospital and treatment. The quick arrival of patients after incidents also meant that we had a high mortality rate — many patients reached the hospital alive who would have died at the scene or in transit if the hospital hadn't been so close to the battle zone. During the 1970s, our expertise in dealing with civil disturbance casualties grew and many doctors and nurses came to us for experience from all over the world. Although the vast majority of the work we carried out in the department was not conflict-related, even during the worst years, it is true to say that staff at the Royal, and colleagues in hospitals across Northern Ireland, did have specialist knowledge that others could learn from. As well as the visits to our department by medical staff from other countries, members of our staff, including myself (see chapter 17), attended conferences in different parts of the world, where they gave papers on the "Belfast Experience".

Although explosions were sporadic, the terrible carnage they caused meant that they were remembered most sharply by the public. However, there were a great many more riots and shooting incidents, which were responsible for the majority of the casualties. I remember a soldier brought into the department; his spinal cord was severed with gunshot and he would never walk again. I said to his pal that I would rather be dead; his pal replied quietly that he would rather be paralysed and alive with his family than dead.

Gun battles occasionally spread into the grounds of the hospital, and even into the building itself. One evening a colleague's retirement party ended with a gun battle. Staff Nurse Rosalie McKinstry had worked for about thirty years on night duty in casualty, in both the old and new departments. Kinky, as she was better known (there was many a raised eyebrow when we called her by that name), was an extremely hardworking and competent nurse, and I was always glad when she was on duty with me. She had trained more doctors than the professors — as a matter of fact, she had trained some of the professors as well. She was especially good with drunken patients, and patients who had taken drug overdoses. On nights, when we were clear of patients, we'd get the chairs from the waiting room and sit down to chat, but Kinky would often fall asleep. One night she was fast asleep in the office when Miss Gaw came down to make a phone call. Kinky slept on. Miss Gaw remarked that I should write in my report for that night, "Kinky slept well."

On the night of her party, some of us had left the celebrations on Level 3 for a quick chat with the night staff in the casualty department below. At that moment a gun battle started outside the entrance door. Two of our nurses had just gone out and they swiftly took cover, lying on the ground between two pillars. Two more nurses lay in the car park between rows of cars. Prisoners and security personnel were guarded when they were patients in the hospital and the guards were changed regularly outside our door; someone had opened fire on them. The first bullet came through our window and embedded in the wall outside the resuscitation room. A policeman was shot outside and brought into us. We had to treat him in the dark as we'd had to put out all the lights when the shooting started. Two staff nurses crawled on all fours, in their party finery, to get equipment to resuscitate him. The casualty doctor put up an infusion in the corridor and the patient was rushed to one of the wards for further treatment. The only casualties among the nurses were the two staff nurses, who had collided in the dark. The Royal College of Nursing representatives and Miss Robb came down to the department the next morning to make sure that we were all right; others were more interested in visiting the bullet hole in the wall of the resuscitation room.

On another occasion, shots were fired inside the resuscitation room. We were treating a soldier who did not have the safety catch on his gun and it went off. The bullet ricocheted and hit the orderly in the foot, but thankfully no one was seriously hurt.

We received many casualties as a result of injuries caused by rubber bullets and the plastic baton rounds that replaced them. Mr Rutherford and some of the other surgeons condemned the use of either, warning the security forces that a strike to the head or body with these weapons was likely to result in death or very serious injury. The surgeons were assured that the use of these bullets would be restricted to hitting people on the arm or leg. This restriction was frequently disregarded. Many thousands of rubber and plastic bullets have been fired in Northern Ireland. Seventeen people have been killed, including eight children. All but one were Catholic. Many others have been injured, some seriously.

Emily Groves was blinded by a rubber bullet as she stood at a window in her home. The bullet hit her directly on the face, damaging both her eyes beyond repair. She had a large family; one of her daughters was a nurse in the City Hospital. Here was a housewife and mother, in what should have been the safety of her own home, suffering this terrible injury. Understandably, she became very depressed when she realised the extent of her injuries. Her family were wonderful, though, and made her the centre of their lives, and gradually she got back her independence. She has travelled all over the world, talking about the dangers of plastic bullets and the callous irresponsibility shown in the use of them.

Many years later I was at a social event. I noticed an elegant lady with dark glasses, dancing and thoroughly enjoying herself. I asked who she was. When I was told it was Emily Groves, I introduced myself to her, and told her that I had been in casualty the day she was brought in. She had had extensive plastic surgery and there was very little scarring. Apart from her eyes, you would not have known she had suffered such horrific injuries. She was an example to all. I do not know if I could have done so much good and got on with my life so successfully. She was a wonderful woman.

Victims of paramilitary-style punishments also arrived at casualty. We became accustomed to looking after people who had been tarred and feathered, for example. The "tar" was usually thick diesel oil, and we used Swarfiga to remove it. The hospital pharmacist used to tell us off, saying that we were using more Swarfiga than any other department in the British Isles, but, then, we were the only department looking after people who had been tarred and feathered. We also used eucalyptus oil. A victim once came in covered with paint, so we asked the hospital painters to advise us on the best way to remove it.

Punishment beatings and shootings, and knee-cappings, were far more serious than people realised. They were terrifying for victims, and upsetting for the hospital staff whose job it was to treat them. These were never simple cases to treat. Some victims died from severed arteries and others had to have limbs amputated in hospital as a result of their injuries. The vast majority suffered damage to their bones and nerves which affected them for the rest of their lives. We once treated a young man who had had his knee drilled with a Black & Decker power drill, which was a particularly horrifying incident.

The Royal was home to many medical advances, developed as a result of injuries inflicted on patients during the Troubles. Out of all the bad came at least some good.

The Belfast external fixator was designed by John Templeton, orthopaedic consultant, and James Mackie and Sons, and used for fractures of the long bones of the arm and leg. The fixator treated the fracture but allowed the treatment of vascular and muscular injuries, and the repair of skin tissue to continue, unlike a cast. The titanium plate was invented by the neurosurgeons and dentists. It was used to cover large skull defects caused by bullets and explosions. The plate was manufactured to fit the defect and screwed into place. Once fitted, the patient soon became used to it. It is still widely used, often on patients injured in road traffic accidents.

I have been asked on many occasions how we nursed members of paramilitary organisations and security forces side by side. One day we had a patient in our resuscitation room who had been shot and needed urgent attention, and in another cubicle we had the gunman who had shot him. I always answer that they all became patients the moment they came through our doors. The only knowledge we required was information that would help us in assessing and treating their injuries. The only priority was that the most seriously injured was treated first. We only nursed patients, in other words, and anyone who had a problem with that should not have been nursing.

Coping with stress

I am often asked how we coped with all the horrific sights and violent incidents we had to endure during those bad years. I reply that, even in the worst days of the Troubles, conflict-related cases accounted for only 1.9 per cent of our work. The rest of the time we were just like any other casualty department, treating patients suffering medical and surgical emergencies, and victims of road traffic accidents. They all had to be looked after. It was no good having a patient with a heart attack quietly expiring in the corner while you were dealing with the casualties of a bomb explosion.

But thinking back to those awful days, I do sometimes wonder how we managed. I think it came down to a dedicated staff and great team spirit. I had great support especially from the sisters and all the nurses. All relevant staff were on standby, though in an emergency it could take some time for them to reach the hospital. But nurses would arrive in from the nurses' home and other staff came in the moment they heard an explosion. As a result, we were never short of nurses, and the rate of absenteeism was very low.

There are many ways of coping with stress in the aftermath of a disaster. We felt it helped us to talk things over with someone who had experienced the same situation. After an incident student nurses, porters, clerical staff, consultants, social workers, trained nurses and domestic staff all sat down together to talk, all of equal importance.

After a traumatic day, no student nurse ever went back alone to her bedroom in the nurses' home. The staff nurses looked after their juniors, both in the department and off duty, taking them to their rooms, if necessary, and staying with them until they felt calm. Mr Rutherford would say of the student nurses in our department in the early seventies: "They came to us very young, but they grew up very fast." At eighteen years old, they would arrive in the department, as many as six at a time, and adapt to the hectic pace quickly and efficiently. When I spoke at a nursing conference in Plymouth, there was general astonishment that we had such young nurses working in casualty, especially in Belfast.

I remember one young nurse starting to cry when she was attending a soldier who had been shot and was critically injured; she had to leave the resuscitation room. Helen went out after her and it emerged that her father had been shot dead some months before. She composed herself and returned to the resuscitation room, and continued to minister to the wounded soldier. She was an excellent and caring nurse. In all the bad years we had only one nurse who had to go off duty because she was so emotionally traumatised by the work in casualty.

As well as coping with our own stress, we had to help patients who were themselves suffering from stress. Many patients who came into the department in the early seventies had been involved in two or three explosions, especially young women working in downtown offices. They were not physically injured but would come in to us screaming or crying or mute. In a psychiatric review of such patients, it was found that many feared going in to town, would not walk past parked cars, became irritable and had sudden and exaggerated reaction to noise. Some smoked more or drank more.

We also had to cope with the danger to ourselves travelling to and from the hospital. The hospital was situated in an area notorious for civil disorder. Gun battles often raged round the hospital, as well as in the grounds and the building itself. One night, Staff Nurse McKinstry and I had to crawl back from our tea break in Bostock restaurant. There was a gun battle in the grounds and the outer wall of the corridor consisted of glass windows. When we returned to the department, I asked the Catholic chaplain, Father Rory McDonald, for the last rites. He said that he would only administer them in a war situation. I said, "What do you think this is?" He slept in the hospital every night, as he was so frequently called to the casualty department.

Members of staff were shot in the hospital. Robin Shields, a former police reservist, was shot dead at his desk in the ambulance depot in 1980. Many years before, Robin had explained how he and a colleague had crawled through a gun battle to go to the aid of a wounded soldier. He little thought he would be shot himself sitting at his work.

Father McDonald died of leukaemia after a short illness and he and Robin Shields were buried on the same day. I went to Downpatrick for Father McDonald's funeral with another nurse, Colette, and we then returned to Belfast to go to Roselawn for Robin's. But bomb scares across the city disrupted the funeral completely — very few of us were able to get there in time. Belfast was at a standstill.

There were frequent checkpoints around the hospital, both checks by the security forces and blocks set up by paramilitaries, and sometimes staff had to drive around burning cars to get to work. At times of high tension and civil disturbance I often slept in the hospital, getting a bed anywhere I could, using the hospital nightdresses and dressing gowns — definitely a vision of loveliness as I walked down the corridor to the bathroom.

One day gunmen came into the department and told the staff and patients not to move while two of their colleagues went to the intensive care unit to attack a policeman and soldier standing guard there. On another occasion, a gunman was in the corridor of our department. One of our doctors continued to move in and out of the minor injury cubicles, treating patients. When the gunman left, we told the doctor how brave he had been. "What?" he said. "What happened?" He had not been aware of any gunman. Mr Rutherford had also continued going about his business, totally unaware of any danger or threat.

At the height of the Troubles, we were frequently so busy treating casualties who had arrived into the department within ten or twenty minutes of receiving their injuries that we did not have time to find out what was going on outside. We were always anxious about our families and homes, constantly worried in case someone we knew would come in injured or dead. This did happen to many members of staff. One time we had a message from ambulance control informing us that two policemen had been shot. One of our receptionists was going out that evening for a birthday dinner with her policeman boyfriend. She said that as soon as she heard the message, she knew he was one of them. Sadly, she was right. Both policemen were dead when they arrived at the Royal. And, as mentioned earlier, Dr Bereen worked in theatre treating casualties of the Abercorn disaster, unaware that his daughter Janet had been killed in the explosion. Around the time of internment the department was inundated with casualties, night and day, and we were rushed off our feet. I was in the department all night.

I invited Reverend Sidney Callaghan from the Samaritans to talk to our casualty nurses and staff from intensive care about how to cope with and care for bereaved relatives. We met in the sisters" sitting room in the West Wing. Reverend Callaghan was a very relaxed speaker, sitting casually in an armchair. He gave an excellent talk, and I have always remembered his key points. He warned us against feeling obliged to fill gaps in conversation; we should wait and listen to relatives. We should never say, "I know how you feel' — how could we possibly know, unless we had had the same experience? And he also said that people often offer a cup of tea just so that they have something to do, not necessarily because it is the best thing for the relatives. I always believed that bereaved people who cried, shouted or even screamed coped better in later life than those who remained quiet.

The Ulster sense of humour was a big help in enabling us to cope, both on and off duty. We had parties for engagements, staff coming and going, and promotions; in fact any excuse would do. Mr Rutherford used to say that to become a staff nurse in casualty you had to be good at organising parties. In 1973 I was awarded the MBE, which I always saw as an honour for the whole department, certainly not as an award for me personally. As an Irish Catholic, receiving an MBE wasn't quite the same for me as for other colleagues at the Royal from the Protestant tradition who received honours at the same time, but I never received any negative reaction about it, and the staff from the department took great pride in the award. They threw a great party and bought me a hat for my visit to the palace. Unfortunately, though, because I heard about the award in June but didn't go to London until November, the hat wasn't suitable, but it was a fantastic present.

We played hockey against other hospital teams, very rough affairs, and all very serious. I was no hockey player, but I was put in goal. Weighed down by my kit, it took me the whole half-time interval to walk from one goal to the other. We put on concerts from time to time and Christmas pantomimes, though we rehearsed very little, as the doctors and nurses were rarely off duty at the same time. I remember performing a not-so-typical casualty scene to the music of *Swan Lake*. Helen and I were dressed as domestics with turbans and rollers. We came in to the "Dance of the Cygnets", with our mops. The two male orderlies appeared as the ugly sisters, decked out in red dresses. The finale was a striptease by two doctors, choreographed with the help of a patient, who happened to be a professional stripper. In one of our concerts, four male doctors danced with three nurses and one female doctor, all dressed appropriately for a risqué French café scene. A picture appeared in the *Belfast Telegraph* and one of the nurses was worried about the reaction of her clergyman father and his parishioners, but we heard that they enjoyed it.

We had wine and cheese evenings, and discos, which were a great success. There were quizzes and panel games, like "Give Us a Clue", between different departments of the hospital, and every year we had a very enjoyable Christmas dinner.

Despite all these entertainments and distractions, there were of course many nights when stress got the better of us, and we did not sleep well. You came to know when you had to get away from the job, even for just a few hours. The nurses often had to be sent off duty, reluctant as they were to leave their patients or go home if it looked like trouble might break out. An important part of my job was recognising when the staff had reached their limits and sending them off duty. A nervous, bad-tempered martyr was of no use to anyone.

My friend Aileen and I would go to the seaside at Holywood or Bangor and walk along the front, even for only a few hours in the afternoon. She lived on the shores of Lough Erne, near Belleek, and I spent many enjoyable holidays there. She needed the break especially, as she lived in the Broadway Towers nurses' home, close to the hospital. The army was based at the top of the towers, and during their frequent gun battles with the IRA, bullets would hit the building. I was in Aileen's flat one afternoon when a gun battle started. We had to lie on the floor until it was safe to move. For a time, the nurses also had to contend with the army being based in Bostock House, the nurses' home on the Falls Road. One nurse came to me and complained that they couldn't go to the bathroom or a friend's room without encountering a soldier. I informed Nursing Administration — I was sure the nurses' parents would not have approved of the situation.

To unwind, I also went across the border for breaks — to Omeath, Buncrana and Dublin. The nurses were offered the use of a cottage in County Antrim and free weekends at the Slieve Donard in Newcastle. Our colleagues in England offered to come to Belfast to help us and we were invited over for holidays.

Support from above is very important. The arrival of managers when the department is coping with a massive intake of patients can be either a good thing or a disaster in itself. Our matron Miss Kathleen Robb was always a great help — in times of crisis she would answer phone calls and deal with relatives. But on one occasion, a certain nursing officer with no emergency experience came down to the department in the middle of a disaster situation and attempted to take over. She redirected casualties, and we ended up with patients with minor injuries in the major cubicles and nowhere to put our seriously ill patients. I phoned Matron and told her that if the nursing officer was not removed, I would resign. I sat outside the office on a wheelchair and watched the chaos. But I could not bear to watch for long, and I soon took over from her. The next morning Matron called me to her office. "Well, are you going or staying?" she asked. I said I was staying. That was the end of that.

I do believe that although we are living in more peaceful times, working in a hospital today can be more stressful in a different way. In my time the professionals were in charge; they knew what they were doing, and they were allowed to do it. As a rule, there was no interference from inexperienced managers. There was excellent co-operation between all departments and we had great help from the hospital's PR consultant, Gerry Carson. When we had a large number of relatives or the press outside the department, I just had to phone him and he would come down and deal with them. We would phone theatre to let them know there were a lot of patients in the department and that the first of them would be up for their operations in a few minutes. There was never any panic, just: "OK, we will be ready."

Resuscitated patients were moved to the wards, theatres or the intensive care unit. Staff there would then take over — by no means was it a question of only our department coping, the whole hospital operated as one big unit, working together for the good of the patient.

World media at the Royal

At the start of the Troubles journalists were not allowed to set foot in the Royal's A & E department to talk to staff or patients, and photographers were not allowed to take pictures. Then Alf McCreary from the *Belfast Telegraph* was given leave to do a series of articles on the department and the theatres, and after that we had an influx of media people from all over the world.

We were well used to people visiting the department, of course. At one stage we were having so many visitors that Dr Gray remarked that we must be on the Tourist Board list of attractions. Every new army General Officer Commanding, every Archbishop of Canterbury, government minister and lord mayor — every VIP, even those of minimal importance — they all came visiting. When we were expecting a visitor, I did not inform the staff — I felt that people had to take us the way they found us.

I find it annoying to see television pictures of seriously injured patients and distressed relatives in hospital. There is a time and a place for cameras and it is not in an A & E department, unless carefully handled and with the permission of patients, staff and

100

authorities. Our security personnel kept all unauthorised journalists out of the department, and Gerry Carson was always a great help in dealing with the media.

Having said that, I generally found members of the press and television companies friendly, professional and in no way intrusive, only doing their job. Some television crews had to sit around waiting for action; one German crew waited for a week and was most disappointed when there was nothing of interest to cover. Some of the nurses suggested filming some of our beautiful Northern Irish scenery, but this would be of no interest to their viewers, they said — what was needed was coverage of the conflict.

A German television crew (from the channel ZDF) made a documentary about our department; they were with us for one week and got on well with everyone. One night they filmed the changing of the guard at the casualty door and were promptly arrested and taken to Hastings Street police station. I had to phone Gerry to get them released. Some nights they slept in our observation ward and gave the domestics a fright when they came into work in the morning. They gave us a party in the King Edward building dining room before they left, and Norma Grindle, who by this time was a sister, wrote a song in memory of their visit, including their arrest. They sent us a tape of their programme and it appeared to me that every time they passed a bombed out building they mentioned my name. I have no German, so I was intrigued — it was as if I was responsible. They went straight from the Europa Hotel — the most bombed hotel in the world at that time —

to Iran, just after Ayatollah Khomeini came to power. We got a letter from them bemoaning the fact that all the alcohol in their hotel had been confiscated and poured down the drains. Not like Belfast then.

Robin Wylie's *Surgery of Violence* which was shown on BBC1 in 1976 received great reviews in all the papers. The central part of this documentary took place in our department. It featured a woman brought into our resuscitation room complaining of chest pain. Nothing much showed on initial examination, but an X-ray showed a bullet lodged in her chest. There had been shooting in her street but she did not realise she had been hit. I do not know who was more surprised — the patient or the staff. As she was being wheeled away to the ward and theatre she was heard to say: "Are they going to keep me in?"

Frank Stagg, a republican prisoner in England, died that day (12 February 1976) after sixty-two days on hunger strike. We had developed a second sense about impending trouble, and decided to stay on duty after 8.30p.m. in case something should happen. The film crew was in the King Edward building, having something to eat. Ambulance Control phoned to say there had been an explosion and they were bringing in some casualties — we told Robin and his team to hurry down.

The central part of the documentary was about a young man who was rushed into our resuscitation room. He had been near a bomb when it went off, and his injuries were horrific. We cut off his clothes, intravenous infusions were started and the doctors examined him. It was obvious he was badly hurt. His eyes had been damaged, which I think must be one of the worst kinds of injury. His wife, Geraldine, was a member of the Royal's restaurant staff and someone fetched her from home. We were all very fond of her — she was always very pleasant and helpful — and we knew she had a young child. As time went on, we knew we were not going to save her husband. Geraldine saw him before he went up to theatre and the priest anointed him. He died later. When Robin's documentary was shown on television, I was worried about the effect it would have on Geraldine, but she said it had been a comfort to see how many people had desperately tried to save his life.

The other people brought in that night were not seriously injured. In the documentary it appeared as if we had a large number of casualties but in all we had only eight, with one critical. On the screen, it looked like organised chaos; I was compared to a sergeant-major in a review of the programme in one of the Sunday papers. Richard Ayres interviewed us after we had cleared the department and were sitting down with cups of tea. One of our young female doctors was literally shaking all over — she had performed well with Mr Rutherford's support during the emergency, but now it was hitting us all. She remarked that only in the Royal would she get such experience. That was true, and unfortunately she would cope with very many more such incidents. Another bomb went off while our professor of surgery was being interviewed, and the explosion was audible in the background. Ayres asked,

"Was that an explosion?" The doctor nodded and went on talking. Just an everyday occurrence.

I had letters from all over the world when this documentary was shown. I received a letter from a nurse who had worked with me in the Royal, but who was by then working in Canada. She was in her kitchen when she heard my voice on her television. She rushed through and was astonished to see me on the screen. Her colleagues had thought our hospitals were old and out of date. The next day they were all congratulating her on having worked in such a wonderful hospital.

At the time of the republican hunger strike in the Maze prison in 1981, we were very busy, and the city felt very tense. I took a call from the receptionist to say that a crew from the American television company CBS was in our reception area. No media people were allowed in the hospital without prior permission, so I went to reception and told them to leave. They said they had had more trouble from me than they had had in their whole time in Vietnam. Later one of them was injured by a plastic bullet, so one of the team finally got into the department, but only as a patient.

One of the most important interviews I gave was published in the *Medical Student*. Joe McGoldrick, now an eminent cardiac surgeon, was the interviewer. The matron of the day, Miss Heather Barrett, had questioned the wisdom of giving this interview because, she claimed, the *Medical Student*, like all student magazines, did not have a good reputation. However, Joe was a very skilled questioner and it was a good article, covering why I liked working in A & E, my opinions of doctors and medical students, and how I felt about the publicity the department was receiving. When he worked with us in A & E a few years later, he was an excellent doctor but also good fun to work with. I saw him years later on the *999* television programme. He was assisting at a road traffic accident; the patient later required his expertise in theatre. I wrote to congratulate him, saying he had not changed much, still looking as mischievous as ever.

Some other short documentaries were made by Ulster Television, in the eye theatre, the orthopaedic theatre, our department, and other parts of the hospital. We were invited to previews at the studios. Helen and I watched with interest until it came to the eye operation. We sat in front of the screen with our eyes covered, unable to look. The television people became concerned, wondering how the general public would react if two hardened nurses found their programme unwatchable. But ours was not a usual reaction for nurses, so they had nothing to worry about. Though I suppose it is odd that severed limbs and horrific injuries did not disturb us, yet we could not bear to watch a film of an eye operation.

I gave many interviews after I retired, for newspapers, radio and television, some in the hospital, others at home. I even received from America a copy of a newspaper article about me that had been syndicated across the States, from major city papers to small local ones, and I had not even been interviewed. On the day I retired I was interviewed by Anne Diamond on TV-am. I was very early in town so when I left the studio I decided to do a bit of shopping. In C & A an old woman approached me, saying how much she had enjoyed the interview. I was beginning to feel like a celebrity.

United Nations nurse — Gaza and the West Bank

In 1989, after my retirement, I was invited to go to Gaza and the West Bank as part of a World Health Organization (WHO) delegation, under the auspices of the United Nations Relief and Works Agency (UNRWA) for Palestine refugees. Our brief was to assess the emergency facilities in hospitals, health centres and the refugee camps available to Palestinians during the intifada, which began in 1987. The delegation consisted of Mads Gilbert, an anaesthetist from Tromso, Norway; Robert Giel, a psychiatrist from Holland; Bill Spier, a retired traumatologist from Munich; and Swee Chai Ang from Malaysia, who had been an orthopaedic surgeon in England before devoting her life to the care of the Palestinians. I was the only nurse.

The doctors had all worked for the UN previously. Mads had worked in Palestine; Bill had worked all over the world for the organisation. Swee Ang was working in a hospital in Beirut at the time of the Israeli attacks in 1982. She was on duty when women and children from Beirut's Sabra and Shatila refugee camps arrived at the hospital, begging to be given shelter as they no longer felt safe in the camps. The hospital was full, bodies were piled up in the morgue, patients were in the corridors, so the women had to return to the camps. That night the women and children were massacred, some tortured and mutilated, by Lebanese Christian militiamen, while Israeli troops stood by, having blocked all roads to the camps. Swee went into the camps the next morning and saw at first hand the horrific scenes. Her eyewitness account was published in her book *From Beirut to Jerusalem* (1989). She is a founder member of the charity Medical Aid for Palestine (MAP) and since the Sabra-Shatila massacres has worked in Lebanon, Gaza and the West Bank.

Robert, very cool and meticulous, became the leader of our group. We were each allocated a particular area to investigate: Mads, theatres and anaesthetics; Bill, the transportation of patients; I had to assess the nursing; Swee examined facilities in the health centres and the general conditions of the hospitals. Robert considered the psychological effect of the intifada on the population.

We stayed at the American Colony Hotel in Jerusalem, a lovely place that had once belonged to a pasha. We breakfasted each morning about eight o'clock, before travelling to the designated areas in a UN van. We would return for dinner around six, then have a debriefing session and write our reports.

The Israeli health minister had forbidden us to contact our Israeli colleagues, and we were refused permission to visit any state-run hospital. We visited nearly all the refugee camps in Gaza and the West Bank and the Arab hospitals. We also visited the hospital run by the Lutheran Church, and the ophthalmic hospital run by the St John's Order in Jerusalem.

The contrast between conditions in the refugee camps and the luxury we enjoyed in the hotel could not have been greater. Following the takeover of Palestinian land and homes by Israeli forces, the UN had set up the camps: concrete shelters, enclosed within a wall, with one entrance, overlooked by an Israeli army post. Over the years, bathrooms and kitchens had been added to each shelter/house. In some camps there were open sewers, while overhead lines of snowy white washing hung on every rooftop — I do not know how the women managed it, given the conditions in which they lived. Doctors, nurses, and professional people lived in the camps, as well as unemployed people and some who were employed in Israel. In one camp I met a cardiac surgeon who had not worked for many years. Some families had owned beautiful homes in other parts of the country, which had been confiscated by the Israelis. They were now forced to live in the camps. We had dinner one night in the home of a well-educated family; they had owned many books until they were removed by the army. Schools had been closed for eighteen months when we were there and teachers who tried to teach in their own homes were arrested.

Large families occupied each small house. The worst time for them was when curfew was imposed, some times for days on end; on one occasion for sixty-four days. People were not allowed to leave their homes, even to go to the doctor or hospital. At such times, the UN distributed food and water. During our stay, some UNWRA medical and nursing staff were trying to get permits to access the camps to visit those in need of care, including pregnant women due to go into labour, and to allow them to transport patients to hospital if necessary. Our delegation met with the Israeli military governor to try to facilitate the issue of these passes. According to him, there was no problem in obtaining these passes, but we knew from our colleagues in UNWRA that this was not the case.

The health centre in each camp was a concrete building, with very few facilities. Midwifery was the most advanced of the available services, and local women were trained to deliver babies in the camps. In the hospitals, about 90 per cent of the nurses were male; in the health centres the nurses were female. Hospital nurses were trained up to Western standards, but the health centre nurses had only eight months' training, more like that of a practical nurse. The nursing colleges were closed permanently. Nurse training was undertaken in Jordan or in the Lutheran hospital.

The only reliable information and statistics at this time were supplied by the UN and MAP, and from the testimonies of delegates like ourselves. We heard that the Israeli forces were using rubber bullets and CS 525 gas, a particularly nasty gas made in the USA, causing, among other things, miscarriages and respiratory problems.

We were gravely concerned about the safety of patients travelling in ambulances. When we were in Jerusalem, we decided to fax a document to WHO, then meeting in Geneva, asking them to censor Israel:

While serving as WHO short-term consultants in Gaza and the West Bank we were shocked by the circumstances prevailing there. For this reason, we take the unusual step of addressing a message directly to you, in the hope that proper action be taken. We found that it frequently is impossible for medical and paramedical personnel to safeguard the rights of their wounded patients to proper treatment against the military. It is becoming customary for them to drag patients from hospitals, clinics or ambulances for investigation, and even to beat them up. Medical personnel and ambulance drivers are threatened and occasionally beaten, while some ambulances have been gunned from close quarters. During curfews health workers have great difficulty in reaching their place of work. We feel that this misbehaviour of the soldiers of one of the member states of the World Health Organisation should be of grave concern to the other members.

This document needed our unanimous support and signatures. Robert's wife was Jewish and he had many friends in Israel. He was first to sign. There are, of course, many good Israeli Jews, doing excellent work with the Palestinians and ashamed of the conduct of their armed forces. One Israeli psychologist we met was carrying out research to ascertain if army brutality would later affect young Israeli soldiers.

Our fax to WHO met with support, and a motion was passed censoring Israel. America abstained and Israel voted against, but other member countries voted for this motion.

We moved from Jerusalem to Gaza, staying in a family-run hotel on the coast, whose guests included journalists, diplomats, nurses, doctors and members of all delegations travelling to the area. This must once have been a lovely place, right on the Mediterranean. There were Palestinian fishing boats, but they were very seldom out fishing, as permits were nearly impossible to obtain. Busloads of people left each morning to work in Israel. A prison camp was situated here; there was not much shelter for the inmates and it must have been cold in the winter and very hot in summer.

In Gaza we visited all refugee camps and health centres, and spent some time in the Ahli Arab hospital, in which Swee had worked. It was the end of Ramadan, when Muslims traditionally visit the graves of their dead. The Israelis, however, had banned the gathering of large crowds, and the people in the cemetery were attacked by the army. Some people were killed and 368 were injured. Mads and Bill went into theatre to help with the casualties; I went to the emergency room but there were enough nurses, all male, and helpers. The matron was an Englishwoman about to retire, and she worked everywhere. In one of the wards the nurse in charge had not been out of the hospital for ten days. He

112

was worried about his family. I stayed to help, although the hospital was so used to this kind of situation that everything ran very smoothly.

There was tremendous noise in the ward, families sitting talking with patients, casualties coming in by all means — ambulances, cars, and some just carried — people shouting. The nurses were very efficient, coping well, obviously very used to doing more emergency procedures than we nurses would at home, and in very basic conditions. The army tried to enter the hospital to question patients but were stopped by the staff. A staff nurse told me how his patients had been beaten in the ward, some even after surgery. UN cars and buses had to be sent out for extra staff and I went with them, driving through the eerily empty streets of Gaza.

On our departure to Vienna I was detained at Tel Aviv airport when I refused to hand over my notes and nearly missed the flight. I insisted the notes were the property of WHO, and eventually they allowed me to board the plane. When we arrived at the UN headquarters, we wrote up our individual reports over a weekend. I do not know if any of our suggestions were implemented; I can only hope they were.

My trip to Palestine made a profound impression on me. During the most stressful times in Belfast, we were able to get out of the hospital and relax in a comfortable home, or even get away for a few days. The Palestinian nurses do not have this option. One of the most lasting memories I have is of the West Bank, when we were driving through Nablus during a curfew. Israeli

113

soldiers were in a bookshop, throwing books into the street and setting fire to them. I could only think of similar scenes in 1930s Nazi Germany.

Conferences worldwide

My first nursing conference took place in England in 1970 and was organised by the Royal College of Nursing. I went with June Fulton, a great orthopaedic sister who died a short time after her retirement. We sat quietly and listened to the presentations, and gradually realised that we covered a wider range of work than most of the speakers and that our newly opened and well-equipped A & E department in Belfast was vastly superior to many others elsewhere. From that moment we started to talk and I haven't stopped since.

I was a founder member of the Accident & Emergency Forum (later Association) of the Royal College of Nursing (RCN) in 1972. In that year it had sixty-six members; by the year 2008 it has at least two thousand members. I chaired the forum for nine years and was secretary for three, and enjoyed terrific support and advice from Margaret Lee, professional officer at the headquarters of the RCN in London. She was a tower of strength and a mine of information; many associations in the RCN owe their very existence to her.

In the early years of the forum the conferences were held in university halls of residence, where the craic was

115

good but the inexpensive accommodation left a lot to be desired. When we graduated to hotel accommodation everyone was happier. Our first international conferences were held jointly with the Casualty Surgeons' Association. The first was held in Tenby, the second one in 1982 in Dún Laoghaire and Belfast. A few doctors took some convincing that nurses could present conference papers, but our colleagues in Northern Ireland were very supportive. We nurses chaired half the sessions and presented half the papers, and one doctor was overheard to say, "We are being shown up here today."

The first paper I gave was at an international combined doctors' and nurses' conference in Plymouth. I was one of two nurses from the Royal who spoke at the conference. I learned a lot both from speaking myself and from listening to the others. When I began my first talk, I turned my back on the audience and spoke to my slides — until the president of the Casualty Surgeons' Association whispered to me to turn and face the audience. Another speaker was unable to answer questions from the floor after her lecture, and a South African professor had to answer them for her. It was always so important to be prepared for questions after your talk.

I was invited to speak at conferences in New Zealand, Australia, Hong Kong, Spain and in many parts of the UK and Ireland. Most of my talks were about my nursing experiences during the Troubles and how we coped with casualties from bomb explosions, riots and gun battles. One year I was asked to give the annual lecture in the College of Surgeons in Dublin to senior members of the nursing profession. After the lecture, matrons, senior tutors and managers approached me with their congratulations. The consensus was that the talk was better than most because I had not used any big words. That was because I did not know any, I told them. I had great help from all my colleagues at the Royal, especially from the staff in the medical illustration department who made my slides.

For my talk in Madrid in 1982, I asked Jackie Carvil, one of the nurses on night duty, to translate the slides text into Spanish. All the Spanish nurses were beautifully turned out and sat with their earphones on, waiting for the simultaneous translation of my talk. However, I tend to speak quickly and the translator had some difficulty keeping up with me. Occasionally I would joke about something, but the time lag meant that the nurses would laugh when I had moved on to describe some dreadful injury. It was very disconcerting. The translator eventually caught up when I had the good sense to slow down.

The Hong Kong conference in 1989 was organised by the Emergency Nursing Foundation of Australia. One of the speakers was an Israeli nurse from Haifa. In my paper, I intended to include my experiences in the West Bank and Gaza. I reckoned she might not be too pleased with what I had to say so I told her in advance about the content of my talk. I thought she might ask some questions at the end, since I had I criticised the treatment of Palestinians, but she said nothing.

The RCN recommended me as a speaker for a conference to be attended by critical care professionals in Auckland in 1981, organised by the Critical Care Nurses' Association of New Zealand. I was the first non-American nurse to speak at this conference; the other two speakers were Professor Donald Trunkey, then chief of surgery at San Francisco General, and Professor Peter Safar, the inventor of cardiopulmonary resuscitation. I was asked to give three papers: two short, fifteen-minute papers on "Penetrating Head Injuries" and "Chest Injuries due to Explosions", and an hour-long lecture on "The Belfast Experience". I feel confident enough talking about my own experiences in Belfast but I had a lot of preparation to do for the other two papers. For the first, I consulted with the staff of the neurosurgical unit and received a lot of help from the nursing officer, Ann Murdoch, and the neurosurgeons. My work in this unit during my student days and my experience of head injuries in casualty meant that this paper was not too difficult to put together. For my chest injury paper, I sought help from my colleagues in intensive care, including Sister Eleanor Hayes, and the two consultants, Dr Dennis Coppel and Dr Bob Gray. I kept this topic as simple as possible, in case I had to field questions from the floor. The staff in the medical illustration department again supplied my slides and were happy to see me go as I had given them so much work to do.

I asked the organisers for an around-the-world air ticket, which was the same price as a return to Auckland. This gave me an opportunity to give my

Belfast Experience paper at hospitals in Perth and Melbourne on route, then attend the conference in Auckland and give talks at hospitals in Wellington and Hastings, before travelling to the States to visit my family in Boston.

I arrived in Perth in the small hours of the morning and was met by the sister from the intensive care unit. My room in the doctors' quarters was very comfortable. An old friend, Phyllis Gilpin, with whom I had trained at the Royal, had left a message of welcome for me. She was at the talk the next day and took me to her home afterwards. We had a great deal to catch up on and very little time to do it in, as I had to catch my flight to Melbourne that night.

Sister Meredith Spencer met me off the plane, took me to her flat, gave me a key and told me to make myself at home. I was exhausted and gratefully accepted her hospitality. Miss Elliott had retired to Australia and we had arranged to meet the next day; my old matron was taking me to a large sheep station, where an ex-Royal nurse was working. But first, I had to give a radio interview.

I had agreed to the interview on condition that I would not be asked any political questions. It was the time of the hunger strike back home, in the course of which ten republican prisoners starved to death in the Maze prison. The first question, however, was: what did I think about the hunger strike? I said it was a tragic loss of young lives. Next, what did the IRA think about it? I replied that I did not know what the IRA thought. Next, how did we nurse members of paramilitary

119

groups and victims side by side? I answered that we did not nurse paramilitaries and victims, we only nursed patients. That ended that.

Miss Elliott had heard this broadcast and she told me she was proud of my answers. She called for me with her friend and we had a wonderful day. I never thought in my days as a student nurse that I would be having such an enjoyable time in the company of the matron.

My talk at the hospital in Melbourne the following day went well, and I stayed with friends of friends from Belfast overnight, before travelling to Auckland the next day for the conference proper, where three hundred doctors and nurses were expected to attend.

Faye Lynch, who had invited me to the conference, met me at the airport. I had been a bit nervous about speaking immediately after Professor Trunkey, who is a very expert, fluent speaker. However, my lectures on head injuries and chest injuries were very well received, and everyone stayed for the talk on the Belfast Experience. During my trip, I gave this talk five times in different hospitals and by the time I gave the last one, I nearly had it off by heart.

After lunch at the Mater Hospital in Auckland, where some Irish nuns who were nursing there gave me messages to deliver home, I gave a radio interview, which went a little better than the one in Melbourne, and then I went on to Auckland hospital to speak to staff who could not get to the conference. Then a flight to Wellington, where I spoke at Wellington Hospital, before flying, in a very small plane, to Napier for a

120

study day in Hastings, a beautiful part of North Island with lovely countryside and vineyards. Professor Safar, the inventor of cardiopulmonary resuscitation, was the principal speaker. He was a charming man, but spoke in heavily accented English so was a little difficult to understand. Of course, there had to be a Royal nurse. Sheila McMurray, who emigrated for one year, met and married a New Zealander and now had a nine-month-old son. She had not changed one bit from her days in casualty.

Back to Wellington for another couple of days, all lectures over, and holidays starting in earnest. I travelled back through Auckland, this time staying with old friends from Belfast, Sheila and Brendan O'Malley. I then stayed with a former neighbour, Father Brendan Sherry in Te Aroha, a typical old New Zealand mining town. I then flew via Honolulu and San Francisco to join my family in Boston.

I have spoken at many conferences all over the world, the majority organised by nursing associations, especially the RCN, and made good friends. Many years after I retired I was asked to speak, with the nurse who was in charge of the hospitals at the time of the Omagh bombing in August 1998, to a small group of nurses — a talk by two nurses, the old and the young. This was my last lecture. I am out of nursing and hospital too long now and there have been many changes, both in training and equipment.

Nursing: Then and now

I retired in 1988 after twenty years in A & E, with the nurse's complaint — a bad back, which had troubled me for some time. An eminent orthopaedic consultant had looked at one of my X-rays many years previously and had said that if I were a horse, he would shoot me! I was glad to leave, although I missed all my colleagues at the Royal and the friends I had made in England through the Royal College of Nursing and the conferences I went to.

I enjoy having more time and the chance to pursue hobbies, such as writing and painting. I joined a non-fiction writing class run by the Belfast Institute of Higher and Further Education (BIFHE), where I received lots of help and advice from teacher Hilda McCready and the rest of the class. Unfortunately there are now very few classes of this kind suitable for senior citizens. I also rejoined the ambulance corps of the Order of Malta, covering some functions and teaching first aid. I gave this up when I realised that anyone who needed CPR from me would have to collapse on the bonnet of a car — getting down to floor level to administer mouth-to-mouth resuscitation was no longer possible. I was very proud to be invested as a Dame of the Order at Armagh Cathedral in 1991. I am the first dame from Northern Ireland and my investiture was the first to take place outside Dublin. After the ceremony, there was a reception, and then I went for a holiday to our house in Omeath with relatives and friends.

At the time I retired I could not foresee the end of the Troubles in Northern Ireland, when former enemies would sit down together in government. The perpetrators of many of the incidents covered in these pages are now working for victims' groups, community groups and, above all, for peace. There may not be universal agreement about the way forward, but a power-sharing legislative assembly is in place and the future looks promising.

There have also been big changes in the National Health Service which have impacted on hospitals, not least the Royal, where I was so proud to work. Since I retired, in a bit of a role reversal, I have been both an inpatient and an outpatient at the Mater, Royal and Musgrave Park hospitals. At each of these hospitals, I received first-class treatment from caring, well-educated and hard-working nurses, and from all the other staff I came into contact with. People might think that this was because I was known to the staff, but the vast majority of them didn't know me, and if they found out that I had been in charge of the A & E department at the Royal, they were only interested in what an old girl like me could tell them about the old times. I was also very well looked after by the after hospital care service. My GP is excellent, too — he is both caring and highly professional.

There have been great leaps forward in terms of the appearance at the Royal. The landscaped gardens, murals and new buildings are all a vast improvement. It's sometimes a very different story inside. We hear a lot about dirty hospitals. In my day, the domestics were attached to a specific department and there was always at least one on duty. They felt part of the team and took pride in their work. We also had Matron doing a round of the department every day — and woe betide the domestics if the wards weren't spotless. Today domestics cover much larger areas and have schedules, and although there is an emergency team on call, it can take some time for them to get to where they're needed.

The government has poured money into the NHS but it hasn't gone to the right places. There just seem to be more and more managers, and fewer and fewer nurses. The patients are not feeling the benefit of the increased spending. Many of the Trusts in Northern Ireland gave obscenely large redundancy packages to general managers and chief executives when they were made redundant; money that could have employed many nurses. The hospitals could certainly do with the return of matrons and night superintendents like Miss Elliott and Miss Gaw. We may have been a little afraid of them but they kept us on our toes, and as a result, patients were well looked after, the standard of nursing was high and the wards were spotlessly clean. Today the patient sometimes seems to be the last thing anyone thinks about. I mean the patient as a whole person —

not just a disembodied fractured leg or broken arm that needs attention.

I have mentioned teamwork frequently in the previous chapters. It plays an important role in any department. In my day, as well as the professionals, the domestic and portering staff formed an essential part of our team. They knew how important they were and were proud to be key members of our department. Our porter, for example, was assigned solely to A & E, helping with patients and taking specimens to the lab. Today there is a central pool of porters; they carry walkie-talkies and can be dispatched to any part of the hospital, and are no longer allowed to do some of the jobs they used to perform when I was sister. Porters no longer feel that they are valued members of a team.

On a visit to casualty just a few years ago, I received excellent treatment. Getting to the X-ray department was another matter; it was like an obstacle course, passing patients lying on trolleys in corridors with no privacy. Curtains have replaced walls between cubicles. Lying on my trolley I could hear clearly what was wrong with the patient in the neighbouring cubicle, every personal detail. I do not know how nurses work in these conditions and remain so cheerful. I said as much to someone in the hospital and she replied, "What were your nurses like during the horrific days? They were just the same." But the difference, I didn't want to point out, was that we were working, sometimes having to make do, in extraordinary circumstances. Whereas the crowded, seemingly chaotic conditions in the A & E department appear to be normal, everyday arrangements these days.

Nurses today are much better educated than we were, always studying and obtaining further qualifications, and this is undoubtedly a good thing. After I retired I joined the Friends of the Royal, an organisation which helped to provide patients' comforts that the Trust was not able to fund. The Friends also offered bursaries to members of staff involved in the clinical care of patients, to enable them to go to conferences, courses and seminars, and visit other hospitals. I was always very impressed by the extremely high standard of research and work being done, in fields such as the care of children with cystic fibrosis and mothers with diabetes in the Royal Maternity Hospital. I was also struck by the fact that nurses were trained in and undertaking work, supported by their consultants, that would certainly only have been done by doctors in my day.

Many nurses, however, do not have experience of patient care until the final year of their degree, and when they qualify some do not regard basic jobs, like washing and changing patients, as their responsibility. It is almost beyond belief for me to hear nurses say that these tasks are not part of their job, feeling that they are beneath them. In my day, we did many non-nursing duties — like cleaning beds, lockers and the sluice. Current nurse training would be improved, in my view, by giving students more time in hospital in first year. I believe that some courses are already starting to provide this.

126

As things stand today, I would prefer to be looked after by a nurse of the old guard, one who entered the profession with a desire to look after her patients and trained in basic nursing care in a hospital run by professionals rather than administrators and managers.

So in spite of all the excellent care, and the new buildings and landscaped gardens at the hospitals, I am glad to be out of nursing. I would find it very difficult to work in a hospital today. I am very proud to have trained and worked at the Royal but it alarms me greatly to hear how many senior nurses in all our hospitals are being moved to undertake other duties, or else have been only too glad to retire early. Basic nursing skills are being lost because a high number of nurses are becoming involved in work that takes them outside the practical field. Nursing is a highly-skilled profession and requires many years of training. Morale is low and the teamwork I valued so much has all but gone. Money is, of course, important, and I am glad that nurses are better paid than we were, but it seems that the further the nurses go from the patients, the better the salary they receive. Nurses are better educated and better paid today, but they should never forget why they entered the profession in the first place — to care for the patient.

Acknowledgements

I would especially like to thank Hilda McCready, who was the tutor of the nonfiction class run by BIFHE that I first attended, and also all the other students in all the classes I attended, for their constructive criticism and support. Thanks too to Bronagh Dalzell, who encouraged me to submit my manuscript to Blackstaff; to Josephine O'Neill who put me in touch with Bronagh in the first place; and to Helen Wright, who has been a good support and help to me.

I have been promising to write this book for some time, and it's thanks to constant encouragement from former colleagues at the Royal and elsewhere that it's now being published. I am also very grateful to the enormous number of people with whom I have been in touch with during the writing of this book and who have provided me with facts and additional information.

UNTIL TUESDAY

Luis Carlos Montalván with Bret Witter

Until Tuesday, Luis Carlos Montalván could barely walk half a mile. Until Tuesday, simply riding the subway was a terrifying ordeal. Luis sometimes struggled just to get out of bed. Because Tuesday isn't just any dog; he's a service dog, specially trained to care for his owner. And with his golden coat and sensitive eyes, he's also the kind of dog that you can't help but love. When Captain Montalván retired from seventeen years of service in the US Army, suffering from physical disabilities, agoraphobia and post-traumatic stress disorder, it was Tuesday who brought him back from the brink. This is the story of how a soldier fought back from the devastation of being injured in action, and how an incredible dog became his protector, his companion and, ultimately, his saviour.

THE STAIRCASE GIRLS

Catherine Seymour

For sixteen-year-old Joyce, who lived in one of the poorest streets in Cambridge, the college building she was about to enter represented privilege, wealth, a life she'd never live. As a "bedder", Joyce would be working up and down one of the stone staircases, making the beds of the male students, sweeping floors and dusting desks. She never expected to also find herself mothering, chastising, and sometimes even covering up for "my boys". Bedders like Nance, Maud, Rose, and Audrey endured the Second World War and had to contend with poverty, ill health, and bereavement. They loved, lost, and loved again. But their friendships gave them strength, and their work gave them happiness — and a lasting connection with their charges, some of whom would go on to run the country.